The Public Library of Nashville and Davidson County

COMEBACK

COMEBACK

■

*How Seven Straight-Shooting
CEOs Turned Around
Troubled Companies*

■

MARTIN PURIS

TIMES BUSINESS

RANDOM HOUSE

All rights reserved under International and Pan-American
Copyright Conventions. Published in the United States by
Times Books, a division of Random House, Inc., New York,
and simultaneously in Canada by Random House of
Canada Limited, Toronto.

Library of Congress Cataloging-in-Publication Data

Puris, Martin.
Comeback : how seven straight-shooting CEOs turned
around troubled companies / Martin Puris. —1st. ed.
    p.   cm.
Includes index
ISBN 0-8129-3127-0
1. Corporate turnarounds—Case studies.   2. Chief
executive officers—Case studies.   3. Communication in
management—Case studies.   4. Business ethics—Case
studies.   I. Title.
HD58.8.P87   1999
658.4'063—dc21   98-27592

Random House website address: www.atrandom.com

Printed in the United States of America on acid-free paper

9 8 7 6 5 4 3 2

First Edition

To HARRY EVANS, who said yes.
To JONATHAN KARP, for his inhuman patience.
To PETER EDIDIN, a man with an unusually sharp mind
and an unusually wry sense of humor.
To both the bad and good clients we've worked
with over the years—the former have made us
appreciate the latter.

CONTENTS

COMEBACK

1/A RIDDLE WRAPPED IN A MYSTERY INSIDE AN ENIGMA

This is a book about how leaders lead. It is not a book of theory, since I am not a theoretician and have no ambition of becoming a management guru. Rather, these pages will place you in the company of some world-class business leaders, each of whom has led his company from the brink of failure to new levels of achievement. Learning how they think and work was my way of enlarging my own understanding of the nature of leadership, and my hope, quite simply, is that their example may help you further along that same road.

This is a personal book, one that arose in part from my need to make sense of a specific example of the powerful influence leadership can exert. In this case, I was the one being led, and perhaps the best place to start our journey through the subject is with this story. Late in 1991, I met Eckhard Pfeiffer for the first time. He had just been named chief executive officer of Compaq Computer Corp., and our advertising firm had just been awarded the Compaq account. It was a large and highly visible assignment, but our competitors were hardly rending their clothes with envy over our good fortune. The company, after all, had recently announced its first loss after nine years of spectacular growth and profits. In the shark-infested waters of the personal computer industry, where a moment's weakness is often the immediate prelude to becoming somebody's lunch, the smart money was betting that Compaq would soon become another piece of roadkill littering the high-tech highway.

Pfeiffer, when we met in his Houston offices, looked like a central casting CEO: gray-haired, handsome, conservatively dressed, immaculately groomed. But nothing else was standard issue. In meetings, he spoke little and to the point. There was no bullying or bonhomie. He often appeared lost in thought, but would invariably correct that impression by asking succinct, pertinent questions about the matter on the table. Quietly, but inflexibly, he remained focused on thoroughly exploring whatever problem was at hand, creating a logical strategy to address it and a timetable for execution.

While in Eckhard's company, I had no feeling of being overwhelmed by sheer energy, charisma or intellectual display. Yet, when I returned to New York from Texas, I withdrew all the assets in my pension account, which were fairly substantial, and placed them in Compaq shares. I had never done anything remotely like it before (and haven't since). Nor was this an ostentatious demonstration of loyalty to a new account—indeed, it's unlikely that, other than my wife, anyone knew what I'd done. Rather, Pfeiffer had, without my immediately registering the fact, convinced me that Compaq would thrive. And it did, executing one of the most rapid and successful turnarounds in recent corporate history.

Pfeiffer's effect on me was to impel action, in this case to place my financial future in the hands of a man I barely knew. It was an action that, multiplied many thousands of times, on the part of other investors, colleagues, suppliers, consumers, bankers and industry observers, became the human substance of Compaq's renaissance. This ripple effect, I have come to believe over the years, is the visible trace of the invisible force we call leadership. Relatively few leaders are called upon to win a war or save a company, but whatever their sphere of endeavor, all have this curious effect of enabling those around them, first, to believe in the future, second, to want to help shape it and, third, to feel enriched by the endeavor. As Max Depree, the longtime CEO of the Herman Miller office furniture corporation, put it in his brief, poetically musing book *Leadership Is an Art*, "The first responsibility of a leader is to define reality. The last is to say thank you."

But what is leadership itself, and not just its effects? Certainly, it is a thing whose absence we often lament, whether in the White House, the school house or the corporate suite. And though, to paraphrase former Supreme Court Justice Potter Stewart on pornography, we always know it when we see it, leadership has proven all but impossible to analyze or define, much less teach. People of every stripe have tried, from Wharton PhDs to football coaches, but without any scientifically verifiable results. The recently published *Knowledge Exchange Business Encyclopedia*, for example, restricts its definition of leadership to the "Ability, through personality or organizational muscle, to influence others toward a goal." Unfortunately, that's all the encyclopedia's editors and advisors felt able to assert. As they write, "Beyond that definition, it is hard to say much about leadership that will not be disputed. That is because countless theorists have come up with systems to describe types of leadership and characteristics of good leaders. But no theory of leadership has held up to testing over time."

It's an area, evidently, where would-be authorities should fear to tread. But the fact remains that I have been, if only in functional terms, a leader myself ever since 1973, when Ralph Ammirati and I founded the advertising firm Ammirati Puris, which grew into Ammirati Puris Lintas, or APL, as it's known to industry insiders. In the quarter century since then, we've grown into a company of some eight thousand employees, spread out over fifty-eight countries, with annual billings of over $7 billion. Running this firm has been the great joy and headache of my professional life, a fair portion of which has been devoted to trying to figure out the nature of leadership. After all, to the extent that I can provide this intangible quality to my colleagues, and to the extent that they can offer it to their people, the more flexible, creative, effective and prosperous we are likely to be.

Arguably, the requirement for leadership, and the sort

of vision described by Max Depree, has never been more critical than now, when rapid political, cultural and technological change has left most of us feeling more than a little unmoored. Certainly, in the business world, a higher premium is placed on leadership than at any time since I began my career thirty-some years ago. Change threatens the stability and predictability of markets. Whether you are IBM, GM, Nintendo, or a Korean *chaebol*, the earth is constantly shifting under your feet and may, in fact, open up at any moment. The data bear out this apocalyptic metaphor. For example, of the Fortune 500 companies of 1970, only a third still exist today.

Just since 1996, when I began work on this book, several of the companies I have been studying have changed dramatically. United States Surgical Corp., for example, agreed to be acquired by Tyco International, for roughly $4 billion in stock and assumed debt. Chrysler, of course, created global headlines when it agreed to merge with Germany's Daimler-Benz, as did Compaq after it announced its purchase of Digital Equipment Corp. for $9.6 billion. Adidas, meanwhile, became the world's number two sporting equipment and apparel company after buying Salomon S.A., for $1.4 billion.

Change of this order can be demoralizing. Authors John Micklethwait and Adrian Wooldridge, in their valuable book *The Witch Doctors: Making Sense of the Management Gurus*, cite the research of psychologist Allan Katcher, who asked twenty "senior American executives" what about themselves they most wanted to hide from their subordinates. "In nineteen out of twenty cases," Micklethwait and Wooldridge write, with barely disguised amusement, "the answer was the same. These trembling Chihuahuas . . . groomed throughout their careers to become top dogs . . . feared that their subordinates would learn how inadequate they felt in their jobs."

Presumably these same feelings of helplessness led to the results of a 1995 Bain & Company survey, which concluded that the average American company used roughly thirteen different management techniques. It's a wonder they aren't all suffering from multiple personality disorder. A quick look at the business best-seller lists will give you a sense of the bromides being dispensed to executives. Leadership, we learn, is an "art" or a "science"; it's "war" or "soul"; it's being the "lead dog" or a supportive "follower." Executives need to flow with the Tao, flip adversity into success through jujitsu, or imagine that their employees comprise a basketball squad or a Green Beret unit. Would-be leaders are told to emulate Winston Churchill, Abraham Lincoln, Attila the Hun, Jesus, Captain Jean-Luc Picard, Lao-tzu, Macchiavelli and Special Forces commandos. A large ad placed in the *New York Times Book Review* by a major publisher reads, "Meet Your New Business Consultants: George Washington, Thomas Jefferson, James Madison. Build strong alliances. Be a risk-taker. Travel with the troops. America's founding fathers offer the best ways to build a great nation . . . or your business."

And this mind-bending litany doesn't even touch upon the generally more sober prescriptions of the leading business magazines and academic journals (have you checked recently whether you are a transactional or transformational executive by nature?).

Theory, of course, never maps precisely onto reality, but

in the realm of business leadership, it often seems to have little in common with everyday experience, or even common sense. In practice, any advice can be useful simply because it makes people feel better, which in turn liberates a certain amount of psychic energy to accomplish the tasks at hand. But my own experience has been that the best advice comes from the example of those who have themselves held positions of responsibility. Certainly, the greatest help I've had in learning how to "lead" my own company has come from consistent exposure to the best and worst in men and women similarly situated to myself. This sort of reverse peer review has created a small universe of positive and negative models, which gave me a context within which to situate my own attempts to improve my performance while charting Ammirati Puris Lintas's course through the, alas, tumultuous changes the advertising industry is undergoing.

The aim of this book is to offer readers something approximating my own experience. It's an invitation to spend time with nine prominent and gifted business leaders: Eckhard Pfeiffer of Compaq Computer, Robert Louis-Dreyfus and Christian Tourres of Adidas AG, Leon Hirsch of U.S. Surgical, Oz Nelson of UPS, Robert Eaton and Bob Lutz of Chrysler Corp., Michael Bonsignore of Honeywell, and Gordon Bethune of Continental Airlines. They are a heterogeneous lot, united at first glance only by achievement and their brave (or foolhardy) willingness to expose themselves to the scrutiny of an outside observer. Otherwise, their backgrounds are as disparate as can be imagined. One is a gourmand and the scion of a great European trading dynasty; another was a high-school dropout whose ambitions extended only as far as becoming a car mechanic. One, a "lifer" at one of the most tradition-encrusted companies in the world—a place that a half-century ago looked the same as it looks today—became a grayflannel revolutionary to bring his firm into the communications age. Yet another is a fiercely independent entrepreneur who has struggled to learn the art of management and bring stability to his company.

I determined early on that I wanted to concentrate on CEOs who had guided their companies through major turnarounds and transformations. This was important to me, because it is in such crises that leadership is most urgently required and may exhibit itself in high relief. When *nothing* is left but leadership and vision, you can see more clearly the work that it does.

To halt a corporation's downward inertial momentum and then to reverse its course is a daunting task. Ben Rosen, the dean of venture capitalists and chairman of Compaq's board of directors, has said he believes turnarounds are more difficult to carry out than start-ups. Shoals of good people leave and must be replaced, morale must be maintained or rebuilt in the wake of layoffs and doleful forecasts in the business press. The market itself needs to be convinced that the company has come back from the dead, that back payments will be made up and promised shipments delivered.

Among the seven corporations featured in this book, only Compaq and UPS are associated with my advertising agency, both as longstanding clients. There is a clear risk that my status as a critical observer will be compromised in the reader's mind by including these two companies, but

I've come to know them so well over the years that I felt
the inside knowledge I could bring to describing their transformations outweighed any potential drawbacks. In the
end, they received no special favors.

It would be nice to report that I approached this subject
with a completely open mind, which always helps an au-
thor sound Olympian and infallible. Unfortunately, that
was not the case. In fact, I came to it with a pronounced
bias—a belief that successful executives have at least one
thing in common.

They pursue the truth.

That is the hidden, unifying thread I hoped to find con-
necting the behavior and personalities of those profiled
here. And to my partisan eye, I found it. That isn't to say
that my protagonists are necessarily philosophically in-
clined (perhaps one of the nine is), or that, like the Greek
philosopher Diogenes, they wander the world, lantern in
hand, searching for proof and certitude. Rather, I mean to
suggest that they display a doggedness, even a kind of com-
pulsion, to dig beneath appearances and uncover the true
state of affairs in the area of their enterprise.

This may seem like an odd trait to use as the foundation
for a book about business leadership, but it is bound up
with the rarefied atmosphere within which most CEOs, and
most senior executives in general, exist. CEOs are effectively absolute rulers, though it's considered politically in-
correct to say so in an age of shareholder rights and boards
that appear to have awakened, after long slumber, to their
legal and ethical governance responsibilities. At large,
multinational organizations, the representatives of entire
nations pay court, eager for the investment capital, prestige

and expertise that the chief executive can shower on them. CEOs also hire and fire at will, realizing the financial and professional dreams of some, while denying or even destroying others.

The fact is that CEOs are held responsible for the success or failure of their companies and that their plans are rarely second-guessed or overturned (short of firing) by their directors. It's for this that they are paid enormous and much-criticized sums of money. If they succeed, there is virtually nothing they cannot do, whether it is spending billions on new programs, changing strategic direction, bankrupting towns through layoffs or granting them new life through capital investment.

Unfortunately, with this power (and it exists, in varying degrees, at a company with ten employees as well as one with ten thousand) comes a court and courtiers, muffling layers of self-interest in which CEOs are swaddled, sometimes without their knowledge and often against their will. My first title for this book was *The Fog of War*, the resonant metaphor from von Clausewitz's classic text, *The Art of War*, for the confusion of armed conflict. It seemed an apt description for the experience of the CEO, who is presented a picture of reality—from which he is shielded—that is almost always false. People may wish to flatter him, or spare him unpleasantness, or hide a failure of their own. Their intentions are not always, not even predominantly, malevolent or disingenuous. It's more that power, which proverbially corrupts its holder, does so partly because it distorts his picture of the world by bending the words and acts of those who come near.

The CEO's field of action, the markets over which he

wars against his competitors, is often befogged, quite possibly to the point of distorting his view and impeding his reaction to the changes that are constantly altering the terrain. In fact, the most precious and difficult thing for a CEO to obtain is a clear view of his or her world. How well is my company performing compared to its competitors? How good are we? How good do our customers think we are? How is company morale outside the executive suite? What does the press think of us? Are they right? Why do investing professionals regard us as they do? Are they right? Who are the best people on my staff? Who are the worst? Are good ideas reaching me or are they being screened out? These are the kinds of questions, critical to the future of any company, to which good CEOs must ceaselessly struggle to get honest answers. In a time when survival, not to mention growth, is dependent upon fast responses to rapidly evolving market conditions, or on seeing far enough ahead of events to move into new markets entirely, the only way for leaders to perform ably is through the astute, disciplined and fast reading of the best information.

In my experience, finding the truth is perhaps the most important thing a CEO can do or, conversely, one of the most disastrous things he doesn' do. Moreover, it's a character issue. Do you want to be told the truth or not? One thing is certain: If once you send out the signal that the pleasantly false is preferred to the unpleasantly true, that's all you have to do—the impression lasts forever. I know this from personal experience.

Back in the 1960s, when I was a young copywriter, an account executive began behaving irrationally, promising a client all kinds of creative work and then never mentioning his promises to anybody at the agency. Naturally, the client grew angrier and angrier as the list of unmet promises grew, while those of us who worked on the account couldn't figure out what was wrong, since we felt our work was strong and effective.

When finally I learned what was going on, I went to my boss, the man who ran the agency, and told him that not only did we have trouble with a large account, but that one of his employees seemed to be having serious psychological difficulties. As I tried to explain some of the odd elements of this strange affair, my boss exploded. He refused to accept that things were going poorly and screamed that nothing was wrong, except that I harbored a hidden hatred of all account executives.

Six months later, the account executive entered a mental hospital (honestly, this is a true tale), but I remained at the agency for another six years. And every time my boss said, "How're things going," my answer was, "Fine." I never again told him the truth about anything. Then I started my own business and tried to do a better job running it.

The destructive effects of refusing to hear the truth, much less invite it, is an issue on which, happily, one of the most respected CEOs in the country is my unwitting ally. In 1965, Ken Iverson took a small, dying steel producer named Nuclear Corp., and turned it into Nucor, the most profitable steelmaker in America and probably the most efficient one in the world. Iverson, who says that the two "most fascinating sights to behold are hot metal in motion and a group of people in headlong pursuit of a shared purpose," has written a toughminded business biography called *Plain Talk*, a lot of which concerns the dangers posed to CEOs by their pharaonic position at the apex of the corporate pyramid. Even if your face never graces the cover of one of the big business magazines, Iverson says, "the inordinate credit our society gives top business executives can still skew your perspective. You can be seduced into forgetting how completely dependent you are on the people whom you manage." The next step, he writes, is to assume that you are "the brains" of the company and the only one who can think strategically or make decisions. "Rarely will such managers stoop to solicit an employee's advice . . . or challenge employees to do more than they, the managers themselves, have been able to do," Iverson says. "If you worked for such managers . . . how long would you go on even *trying* to make a difference?"

Even if you send out the right signal, however, the battle for clear sight lines to the world beyond your office never ends (ironically, these are invariably corner offices in skyscrapers with stunning views). The hardest thing in the world for me, beside firing people, is to get the truth—the facts. I worked on George Bush's reelection campaign in 1990, and was struck by how similar in this respect are being President of the United States and the CEO of Widgetronics. By the time Bush ended his time in office, he trusted about three people, all of whom were wrong. His circle of information had grown smaller and smaller, and he had no idea how he was perceived around the country. Corporate CEOs suffer the same fate; they learn first to distrust people, then to dispense with those whose views they find disagreeable. Next, quite often, they decide the press is the *cause* of their troubles, whatever they happen to be. And last they find themselves in a corner, faced with believing they know it all, or realizing that they have lost the market and personnel intelligence to feel confident that they know *anything* that they need to know.

Take two of the great recent corporate disasters: Dr. Wang of Wang Labs and James Robinson at American Express. These are smart guys, so what happened? Why did they fail so dismally? I saw at close range what happened with Bush: He lost touch with the truth almost totally. He let himself be shielded. And you have to say that if James Robinson or Dr. Wang or George Bush had the facts in front of them, they'd make the right decision. They're not dopes. They just became separated from the realities of their own businesses. So did Steven Jobs, an astoundingly creative and intelligent executive, who made every conceivable mistake at Next Computer. Rod Canion, too, had the insight, intelligence and drive to found and lead Compaq, yet committed a sequence of fundamental errors in distribution, pricing and marketing that almost destroyed his own creation. All of these people had sealed themselves off from the world. They saw what they wanted to see and heard what they wanted to hear. They were flying blind and had no idea they were headed for the side of a mountain.

The nine men profiled here are at the opposite end of the executive spectrum. However disparate their backgrounds, personalities, management styles and the businesses they run, each displays a relentless desire, in the judiciously admiring words of one chief legal officer, "to make certain [they] are provided information that is balanced and of the highest quality." At their companies, no one is ever shot for bearing bad news; that risk is reserved for those who knowingly bring false cheer or no news at all, or repeatedly fail to measure up to a high and uniformly applied standard of competence. For the same reason, perhaps, the corporate cultures in this book are unusually collegial, while often extremely competitive at the same time. People are expected to be good. These institutions, in their respect for applied intelligence, are light-years away from the world I glimpsed inside a major retailer, whose CEO told me, "All I need is a gimmick" when describing how he would lead his company from the doldrums to success (he never found one and we declined the account).

Samuel Johnson once said of biography that, "It gives us things we can use" in our own lives. The profiles in this book fall far short of the stately inclusiveness of biography, but they will, I hope, give all who read them things they can use in contemplating their professional lives and in improving them where possible. There is also an optimistic subtext here: These men have achieved every professional success, including the wealth and acclaim that goes along with it, yet they have not been seduced by power and success. They have not forgotten the worth and importance of their colleagues and peers. Moreover, they all arrived at their present eminence via the "high road." These were not careers made by politics and scheming, but overwhelmingly by application and intelligence, demonstrating competence and winning trust.

This is not a statistical accident, in my view. I believe that the truth, taken as a guide to executive behavior, helps to inculcate and reinforce that very old-fashioned thing known as strength of character. And that is something all senior executives, sooner or later, will need. As Ken Iverson puts it, "You have to accept that your operations will stand or fall on their own merits. There's no cavalry waiting to ride in to the rescue. . . . There's just you and those people working with you. Together you'll find a way to succeed. Or you'll fail." That is the truth, and all executives need to learn how to handle it.

In the end, there really aren't any tricks to consistent success in business, or to leadership. I hope this book helps readers to understand why this is so, and that it gives them some of the resources they need to find and hold this quality in themselves.

2/Gordon Bethune
The Mechanic

When Gordon M. Bethune became president and CEO of Continental Airlines on Valentine's Day, 1994, the tall son of a Texas crop duster had, in the opinion of the financial and the aviation press, taken on an unsalvageable mess. Employees, who saw a profane former high school dropout nicknamed "Oil Can" riding to their rescue, agreed.

"Here's a company," Salomon Brothers airline analyst Julius Maldutis dryly noted at the time, "that has some fundamental problems."

Continental had lost money twelve of the sixteen years since the airline industry was deregulated in 1978. And the company had declared bankruptcy twice in the previous decade. Worse, Continental had recently been owned by Francisco (Frank) A. Lorenzo, who was so demanding that one of his subordinates joked that the company's version of carrot-and-stick management was to insert a carrot into the collective posterior of his workers and then hammer it in with a stick. No wonder morale among the airline's forty thousand employees was such that some of them had ripped the company's logo off their uniforms.

"It was the most dysfunctional company I've ever joined," says Bethune, fifty-six. "It was like dealing with abused children. They kind of like you, but everybody else has screwed them for who knows how long, so you've got to gain their trust and confidence."

One Denver employees' meeting in the early days nicely illustrates his point. Facing a room of manifestly skeptical employees, Bethune made a few anodyne opening remarks, before a pilot stood up and bluntly questioned whether Continental could be resuscitated, and if it could, whether Bethune was up to the job. After a few moments of deafening silence, Bethune barked: "The jetway is still attached for you, buddy. You can get off, or you can get on and shut up."

This was pure Bethune—candid, direct and confident—and it worked. In the year following Bethune's arrival, Continental became the first airline ever to jump from last to first in the J. D. Power and Associates ranking for domestic airlines on long-haul flights (one year later, it became the first airline to win the award two years in a row). And after routinely finishing at or near the bottom in the Department of Transportation rankings for late arrivals, lost baggage and customer complaints, it now often finishes in the top quarter. Financial performance has also improved substantially. The carrier has posted record profits, reduced its once-crushing debt and built a cash reserve of over $1 billion, all of which has driven the stock up tenfold in the past two and a half years.

"By all reasonable measures, this was an extreme turnaround," says Marc Knez, an associate professor of strategy at the University of Chicago Graduate School of Business. "Prior to Bethune, few, if any, would have predicted a turnaround of this extent, even taking into consideration that the whole economy is doing better."

Not everyone is applauding. Some former Continental executives, most of whom Bethune unceremoniously terminated, have said off the record he was taking credit for initiatives begun by others. They also note he has benefited from overall improvement in a cyclical business, while industry analysts worry that the cost of replacing Continental's aging fleet—it will buy sixty-four new planes in 1998, and expects to have the youngest domestic fleet by 1999—will jeopardize the company's renaissance.

"All that needs to happen," says Richard D. Gritta, a professor of finance and transportation at the University of Portland, in Portland, Oregon, is for the country to go into recession, or for interest rates to go up sharply, or for inflation to reappear, or fuel prices to rise, or for unions to get more feisty and demand a bigger part of the pie, and then you will see the kind of profits Continental has been posting will disappear as fast as they appeared."

Bethune, however, responds to Continental's current

Cassandras much as he did to that pilot in the dark days of 1994. "Bullshit," he says.

Bethune's current eminence would have been unimaginable to the thirty-six-year-old Lieutenant Gordon Bethune when he left the Navy in 1978, after a twenty-year tour. After all, the last time he'd been a civilian was when he enlisted as an eleventh-grade dropout. "When I was really young," he says, "my father, a crop duster, taught me how to fly an airplane. He wanted me to be a pilot, but like a lot of dumb-shit kids I didn't want to do what he wanted me to do. So, I ran away from home and joined the Navy and became a mechanic."

Bethune wasn't just another grease monkey, however. He was stubborn and smart and, in the most aristocratic and class-conscious of the services, determined to prove himself as good as or better than the next man. The first thing he did was to get his GED (general equivalency diploma). It wasn't good enough. "I said to myself, 'Hey, this is an equivalent, and I don't want to be an equivalent.' So, when I was transferred to Key West, I went down to Key West High School and got my regular high school diploma at night. I hated school as a kid, but I kind of liked this. I liked doing it for myself."

The Navy also taught Bethune that he liked authority and had a gift for exercising it. "They told me how to measure success," he recalls. "They brought me in on their side. I put all my energies into their definition of success; I kept doing more and more, and pretty soon, I was an officer. Then, when I was an officer, I made sure I didn't do the stupid things other officers had done, to make sure that we were successful.

"When I left the Navy, the squadron I ran—the maintenance department—was the best maintenance department in the Navy, recognized by the Chief of Naval Operations. We won the award that year. You know why? Pretty easy. Get those guys to want to do it. And to want to do it, you've got to respect them, and you've got to talk to them in their language."

After leaving the Navy, Bethune intended to enter college and become a lawyer, but an old Navy buddy, Ed Bollinger, had joined Braniff Airways and convinced him to sign on as a maintenance foreman in Dallas. "Gordon has a good sense of the bottom line and also of Weber's Theory," says Bollinger, today an executive at Carnival Cruise Lines. "Weber's Theory says that if you are magnetizing all the molecules together you get them all to go north and south instead of helter-skelter, and that means you get a nice strong magnetic field.

"Managing people is a lot like that. You get them working together—north pole, south pole—and you have more force. That's what teamwork is about—getting everyone working in unison. And that's what Gordon excels at."

At Braniff, Bethune continued his personal and professional ascent, becoming maintenance director and earning a night-school BA in General Studies from Abilene Christian University at Dallas. Later, Bethune taught himself finance, reading textbooks the way a maintenance man might read an engine repair manual. "You can't be the head of a company and not understand the financial implications of what you're doing," he says. "I mean, you've got a couple of hundred million bucks you're spending, and you've got to understand the budgeting process. You have to understand the capital structure of the company. But it's not hard; it's just some shit you read."

One of the early victims of deregulation, Braniff ceased operations in May 1982, and Bethune became vice president of engineering and maintenance at Western Airlines, aka "The Garage," in Los Angeles. There he was nicknamed "Oil Can" by Jerry Grinstein, who later became the CEO of Burlington Northern Santa Fe, the Fort Worth railroad company, and a board member of Delta Air Lines. The moniker was a reference not only to Bethune's background as a mechanic but also his methodical problem-solving abilities and his people skills.

"Bethune's leadership style is uninhibited persistence," Grinstein says. "It might not play well at AT&T or IBM or Chase Bank, but it has served him well at Piedmont, Boeing and now Continental. He picks very bright executives, wades into battle with them and, almost like a Western frontiersman, he fights to win. It takes a lot of self-confidence to lead the way he does."

A short time later, Bethune moved yet again, to become senior vice president of operations at Piedmont Airlines, based in Winston-Salem, North Carolina. For a time, the fastest-growing carrier in the nation, Piedmont merged with USAir in 1987, and Bethune was hired by Boeing—a rare move at a company known for grooming its own executives. "Gordon is one of the world's great communicators," said Ron Woodard, president of the Boeing Commercial Airplane Group, and the number three person in the Boeing organization. "He has an absolutely magnificent way of simplifying things."

Woodard said that Boeing president Phil Condit wanted an airline executive to help support the aircraft manufacturer's customers, so Bethune became vice president and general manager of Boeing's customer service division, and then he took over as general manager of the Renton Division, which built 737s and 757s. Bethune was also the only top executive certified to fly Boeing's equipment. (Bethune has personally flown several new Continental 757s from Boeing's plant in Seattle to Houston.) "When Gordon got his type rating on the 757, he and I chatted about it. He said he had flown lighter planes, but this time he had basically bitten off more than he could chew," Bollinger recalls. "But he had to do it, he had to succeed. So, he just buckled down and in three months did a pretty incredible task. With just a few hundred hours' flight time he got his type rating."

At Boeing, Bethune also completed his personal turnaround by attending Harvard Business School's Advanced Management Program—surely the only member of his class who entered the job market as a high school dropout. "I learned a lot about commodity marketing," he says wryly. "I also learned that out of the 130 people in my class, I was okay. You never know how you fit with the big shots you read about in *Business Week*. Then you go sit with [the] cream of the crop of big shots from around the world, and you find out that you can compete with those guys pretty good. You're okay."

Bethune's odyssey through the airline business had given him a front row seat from which to watch and experience the turmoil that visited the industry after the Carter Administration pushed deregulation through Congress in 1978. Mergers, startups and bankruptcies were the order of the day, and nowhere was this chaos more brutally expressed than at Continental.

From 1936 to 1981, nearly a half century, Continental was the domain of a former silk scarf-and-goggles barnstormer named Robert F. Six. Six was smart, flamboyant, a marketing wizard and a good boss to boot. "Herb Kelleher of Southwest may be the nearest thing we have today to an airline executive like Bob Six," says James R. Ashlock, former airline editor for *Aviation Week & Space Technology* magazine. As with Kelleher, Six's emphasis on service, style and employee involvement gave Continental a distinctive brand image, which helped make it a perennial industry leader in profitability and efficiency.

Like an athlete who knows when to quit, Six retired in 1981, three years after deregulation. No-frills carriers and deep-discount fares proliferated, causing a loss at Continental of $13.2 million in 1979, compared with a profit of $49.2 million in 1978. The company's break-even load factor, once under 40 percent, was suddenly 63 percent of available seats.

In the years following deregulation, recession, high fuel

costs and other factors caused Continental to hemorrhage red ink. A merger with Western Airlines fell through in early 1981 and company morale, once the envy of the industry, crumbled, especially after 1980, when the airline was forced to make its first major layoffs in forty-six years. Then, just before Christmas that same year, the flight attendants struck.

It seemed things could not get any worse, at which point Frank Lorenzo arrived. His hostile takeover raged for months, in courtrooms, state legislatures and even the halls of Congress. The employees, led by Al Feldman, Robert Six's handpicked successor, tried to buy the airline by issuing additional shares to the employee stock option plan. The gambit failed and shortly thereafter, in August 1981, Feldman committed suicide. (Friends said he had been deeply depressed since the death of his wife from cancer a year earlier.)

In 1982, months after Lorenzo took over, he merged Continental with Texas Air, despite having promised never to do so. Still, the combined operation, just like the separate ones, kept losing money. Then, on September 24, 1983, Lorenzo took the company into bankruptcy. Three days later, under court protection, the airline resumed service to twenty-five cities, down from seventy-eight a week earlier. It also cut its payroll from twelve to four thousand. Three days later the pilots' union and the flight attendants' union went on strike. Lorenzo simply hired replacement workers.

While in bankruptcy, one of the longest and most complex in U.S. history, Continental gradually recovered, posting healthy profits in 1984 and 1985, and slowly returning to its prebankruptcy size. Then, in 1986, a few months before Continental exited Chapter 11, Lorenzo and Eastern Airlines Chairman Frank Borman jointly announced that Texas Air was buying troubled Eastern Airlines for $600 million. Wall Street was ecstatic; Eastern Airline's unions, among the most militant in the nation, were not. Confusing the situation even more, Lorenzo quickly bought People Express and Frontier Airlines. The merger of these disparate operations proved to be a logistical and cultural nightmare. Complaints soared at the new cobbled-together Continental Airlines, profits evaporated and amid a storm of vilification and ridicule, Lorenzo sold his stock to Scandinavian Airlines in 1990 and bailed out.

Once again, Continental began to right itself, only to be blindsided by Iraq's invasion of Kuwait, which drove fuel prices from $.57 to $1.40 per gallon almost overnight, forcing the fragile carrier back into bankruptcy on December 3, 1990. Led by Hollis Harris, and then Robert Ferguson III, Continental struggled back to fiscal health for the second time in seven years and emerged once again from Chapter 11 in 1993. In fact, with an infusion of cash from several new investors and having created a separate low-cost no-frills line, CALite, Continental seemed rejuvenated. The company even began restoring employees' back wages.

But the recovery was an illusion, as everybody in the industry knew, including Bethune when he took over in 1994. Continental appeared to be in robust good health. In fact, at one early press conference, Bethune joked that the only reasons he had gotten the job of CEO were that he was "too dumb" to turn it down and nobody else wanted it.

"When Gordon took over the company, I called him and told him that I couldn't congratulate him because he had just stepped into the biggest pile of shit he had ever been in," Bollinger says. "I was joking, but the company was in dire straits. It was so messed up no one else wanted it.

"Still," he adds, "I really had confidence that Gordon, if anyone, could straighten it out. He was the right guy at the right time with the right set of skills. You know, in the Navy, you tend to play poker a lot and life is a lot like poker, in that you are only dealt a certain hand and you have to do the best you can with it. So, playing all that poker must have helped Gordon a lot at Continental. He had a certain hand he had to play, and he just had to do the best he could with what he had."

The problems at the airline were manifold. While other airlines posted record profits for the third quarter 1994, Continental turned in anemic results, below analysts' expectations, and lost money for the year, the company's fifth unprofitable year out of six. Consumer complaints were running two to three times the industry average, and the low-fare Continental Lite was still unprofitable a year after its launch. Continental was slowly bleeding to death.

■

A few months later, having become president and CEO, Bethune began to make his presence felt. The changes were large and small—and ubiquitous. Fridays became casual-dress days, a special access card was no longer required to enter the twentieth floor of Continental's Houston head-quarters (where Bethune's office is located), and he divided his old job as chief operating officer among eight people. "This is all about team-building," he told them.

Well, not all. It was also about bloodletting. Fifty of the company's sixty-one officers were fired. At the same time, Bethune enlisted Gregory D. Brenneman, a thirty-three-year-old wunderkind consultant from Bain & Co. in Boston, to help reorganize the airline.

Bethune and young Brenneman, today Continental's president and chief operating officer, huddled together at the dining room table at Bethune's stately home in Houston's River Oaks section, creating a turnaround manifesto that they called the "Go Forward Plan." "We called it 'Go Forward,'" Bethune remembers, "because I used to say, 'You know why there's no rearview mirrors in the cockpit? Because nobody gives a shit what's behind you.' People were spending too much time on stuff like complaining about what Frank [Lorenzo] did to them."

For his part, Brenneman recalls, "I was living in an apartment and half the time I would go over and eat dinner with him. We literally sat at his dining room table and wrote down everything that was brain-dead about the company—all the things that were screwed up with it.

"We wrote ['Go Forward'] over about three dinners, which we now sort of fondly refer to as our Last Suppers. We honestly didn't know how bad the situation was around here, and if we'd had any inkling about how bad it was, I don't think either of us would have been here."

The plan had four components: "Fly to Win," "Fund the Future," "Make Reliability a Reality" and "Working Together."

"Fly to Win" was the marketing plan and the first part of the recovery strategy, since Continental desperately needed to staunch its quarterly losses. The essence of "Fly to Win," Bethune says, was "stop doing things that lose money; fly to places people want to go; price yourself competitively. Don't compete in markets that you can't dominate, restore the frequent flier program, put first-class seats back on airplanes.

"Our [strategy] was not so much think of new things to do, but do things that had worked and only do things that would make money. So, we looked at cash-negative flying. Fifteen percent of all of our flying was cash-negative, which means you might as well set the parking brake and evacuate the airplane because it's cheaper. And, as a matter of fact, that's what we did. We took a whole fleet of airplanes out that equated to fifteen percent of capacity. And we exited markets where we weren't making any money. People didn't want to go between Greenville, South Carolina, and Greensboro, North Carolina. Didn't want to go. But we flew there six times a day. We stopped it."

Bethune also closed the Los Angeles maintenance facility and laid off 1,500 workers. And he folded CALite. The venture, modeled after Southwest Airline, grew too fast, customer service suffered, loyal fliers were alienated and, the bottom line: revenue failed to meet projections. "I'm not sure it failed because it was a bad idea," he says. "It failed because we had no ability to implement anything."

The second part of the "Go Forward" plan was, if anything, still more critical. On Thanksgiving 1994, Brenneman projected that Continental would be out of cash, out of business, on January 17, 1995. "I called Gordon, and I called the board, and we all sat down and said we've got two options," Brenneman remembers. "One is we can sit down with the eight largest creditors and try and renegotiate this deal, or secondly we can go into bankruptcy for the third time, which no one had ever recovered from. And so, we sat there and looked at both of those choices, and decided we'd sit down and renegotiate with the creditors."

This set the stage for a game of high-stakes chicken. Brenneman called a meeting of all Continental's creditors. "Here's where we're at," he told them. "Here's where we're going to take the company. And here's what we need you to do to help. And if you don't do this, you're leaving us with no alternative."

Many of the lenders and vendors at the table had their careers riding on deals they had made with Continental and, according to Brenneman, "They started yelling at me. I got up to walk out, and they said, 'Greg, where the hell are you going?' And I said, 'I'm going to go home.' And they said, 'How can you come in here and tell us all this stuff and go home?' And I said, 'Do you guys know what the first step in problem-solving is?' They said, 'No,' I said, 'It's determining who has the problem.' I said, 'This whole company's worth a hundred and seventy-five million in equity, and you guys are in the hock for three billion. This isn't my problem. I'm going to go home and watch TV,' " he says, laughing.

"Needless to say, they came out and grabbed me, and we sat down, and we worked out a deal. And they're all paid off now, a hundred cents on the dollar."

It's a good story, but at the time the stakes were high, the future precarious, and everybody was nervous. Larry Kellner, who Bethune hired away from American Savings Bank to be Continental's chief financial officer, arrived at about this time and recalls the day-to-day tension. "We had very little cash and four hundred and ninety million dollars of debt in default," he says. "And we had over a billion dollars of operating leases in default. So, any day when we woke up, somebody could pull the plug on us."

"But," he adds, "nobody was pulling the plug because having us alive was better than having us dead."

Even with the lenders' aid, the airline still needed help, and to get it Bethune turned to his old colleagues at Boeing. Continental had several planes on order, secured with a substantial (and nonrefundable) deposit. "They had sixty million dollars of our money in commitments for those airplanes," Bethune recalls, and he needed it back. So he called Woodard at Boeing and had a brief conversation: "I said, 'I really need those cash deposits back,'" Bethune says. "He said, 'We'll let you have half,' which is more than I thought they would ever let me have. I said, 'Ron, you got to wire it today,' and he laughed and said, 'Okay.'"

Woodard remembers the day vividly. "He called me up and told me, 'Pal, I never ask for something unless I really need it.' I think we got it there at the end of the day.

"I knew Gordon well enough to know that he wouldn't ask if it wasn't important," he adds. "I also know that if I was ever in the soup, Gordon would help, no questions asked."

Indeed, that single phone call in January 1995 may have kept Continental out of a third bankruptcy. "It was critical," Bethune says. "Our cash balance that day was never lower. We weren't going to make payroll. We needed sixteen million dollars. One more week, and we would have been out of business."

Kellner adds, "Sure, we clearly needed help from Boeing and GE and from a couple other people. But even in those darkest hours, they helped primarily because of their belief in Gordon and Gordon's strategy, which is have a good product, and have people want to come to work every day."

The last two parts of the "Go Forward Plan"—"Make Reliability a Reality" and "Working Together"—are related. "We were a very poor operating company, and had been for years," Bethune says. "How can you be number ten for ten years on the DOT customer satisfaction and on-time metrics, and think you're going to be in this business?

"People here were conditioned to fight each other and to hate management. They were winning and losing internally, and not externally. People were getting ahead because I got the budget and you didn't, and you got fired and I didn't, and all these kinds of stupid metrics that don't mean anything."

The "reconditioning" began with the people Bethune and Brenneman hired to replace the executives they'd fired. "We tried to just get smart people in, some of whom had airline experience and some of who didn't," says Brenneman. "We said, 'To work with us, you have to be smart, and you have to be able to work with other people, and to get things done.' "

Woodard notes that Bethune also brought aboard some old hands, people that he could trust, such as C. D. McLean, executive vice president for operations, and George Mason, the senior vice president for technical operations, who worked with Bethune at Piedmont.

"If you look at his management team, there are people

there he has repeatedly gone to war with in the past at Piedmont, at Western," Woodard says. "These are people who have stuck with him. Gordon just has a great way of sniffing out who is a true friend and supporter and who isn't. He told me once that when people are getting their own way they're always nice. You can't really tell about people, though, until they aren't getting their way. That's when the nice people stay nice people, and the jerks become jerks."

Next, Bethune began rewarding every single employee when the airline finished among the top five in on-time performance. They received $65 checks each month for placing third through second, $100 checks for first place. At an airline that a few years before had stopped carrying aspirin onboard just to save $10,000 a year (and you *needed* the aspirin), this was an extremely meaningful gesture.

"The DOT says customer satisfaction measures are: on time, with your bag, general complaints, and don't bump me off the plane involuntarily," Bethune says. "Those are the four metrics. So we measure and reward those. The first month of the program, February 1995, we came in fourth place, and everybody got this check. Sure, it was only sixty-five bucks, [but] you could not imagine the positive reaction when people got those checks. And I wouldn't let them take tax withholding out of them either. Sixty-five bucks."

The bonus program cost $3 million a month, a not-insignificant sum, but that was half what the airline was spending to shuttle passengers onto competitors' flights because of late arrivals, missed connections and other mishaps. More important than the dollars involved, says

Bethune, the bonus checks "have driven a cultural change that says our employees win only when the customer wins; and if the customer loses, we lose.

"In the old days, there was a factionalization," he says. "Let's take the flight attendants at departure time, and we're going to LA. It's Houston. And our caterers are eight meals short. The flight attendant says, 'Hey, buster. I'm not going to LA without any meals. You get me the eight meals.' And he says, 'I don't have them in the bank at the terminal. I have to go back to the kitchen, and that'll be twenty minutes.' She says, 'It's your problem. Get it.'

"Today, eight meals short, she says, 'Don't you do this to me again. All right?' And he won't. She closes the door. And she'll find some journalists that will trade booze for food in the back, to make up for some lost meals. Or she will be short meals. But she'll get the goddamned airplane going in on time because she can only win when we beat American, United and Delta, and not when she beats the caterer. It used to be, well, it's his problem because it was his delay. Now, it's *our* delay."

Sally Pettingill of Houston has been a flight attendant with Continental since 1978. "Gordon is direct," she says. "He has the ability to walk the talk. He is committed, and that gets other people committed. Plus, he treats me like a peer as well as a flight attendant.

"He has improved morale tremendously. He realizes that if you treat people with respect you get the same response. And he realizes that unless the employees are working to make the airline succeed it won't happen. He has also changed the focus of the company—we're now customer-oriented," she says, "we're not some cattle car any more."

Michael Cox, Continental's former treasurer, who worked at the company from 1984 to 1995, agrees with this assessment. "Most of Gordon's predecessors were of a deal-making mentality," he says. "The deal-making mentality overloaded the company with debt, chose several irrational mergers as a strategy for growth, and when the early nineties recession hit, drove Continental into bankruptcy. Gordon was one of the first chief executives of the airline to prioritize areas such as on-time performance, clean air-craft, and the like." In other words, Bethune didn't just want a clean balance sheet, he wanted to run a good airline. It was back to the days of Robert Six.

For this he needed talented and committed employees, so along with the bonuses, the company began paying out on a company-wide profit-sharing plan, which reserved 15 percent of pretax income for employees—no exceptions. It had been sixteen years since there had been any profits to share—so long that most employees weren't even aware that such a plan existed. "Why would employees give a shit about profits as long as their paycheck is good?" Bethune asks. "The answer is—they won't. But now that fifteen cents of every buck the company makes is their buck, guess who's interested? They're all interested."

That goes for the top of the corporate pyramid, too. "The way I reward the top management of the company is they all get a bonus or nobody gets a bonus," Bethune says. "Every three months, we get a bonus, but only when we hit our numbers. And so, if you're engaged in screwing over your buddy over here, we'll probably miss our number, and you won't get paid and neither will he. And even if you get his job, you won't get any more salary. The airline business is, I guess, the biggest team sport in the world. And if you don't know that, you're going to fail at it."

The interesting thing is that Bethune, as he overhauled every element of his airline, wasn't in the least shy about telling people how bad things were and how easily the company could fail. He was utterly straight in this respect. But he projected equal, unwavering confidence that if everyone would pull in the same direction with him and make the changes that needed to be made, Continental would succeed. He told everybody the worst. Then said, in effect, follow me and we'll win. It was an absolutely classic exercise in leadership.

The extent to which Bethune's tenure has changed the culture at Continental can be hard to grasp for an outsider. George Thompson of Houston, a pilot for thirty-two years at Continental, says simply, "Gordon Bethune has worked miracles here. This company would not be here if it were not for Gordon—and I don't kiss butt."

He adds that even in contract negotiations between the pilots and the company, the relationship is now cordial. "We have our differences, but there is a level of trust and respect there now that didn't exist before," he says.

Thompson, who was on strike from 1983 until 1987, even organized an employee appreciation day for Gordon in 1995, and helped raise money to buy him a new Harley Davidson motorcycle. Such a present would have been un- thinkable under some previous Continental administrations. "We actually raised twice as much money as we needed," Thompson says.

Grinstein, now a competitor at Delta, is openly admiring of Bethune's turnaround at Continental. "He is ideal for CAL," he says. "The company lacked direction, strategic force, a sense that it could succeed, and internal collaboration. 'Oil Can' gave it optimism, and with Brenneman developed a strategy and reengineered his workforce. And with a little bit of help from the business cycle he has triggered something remarkable. He gets very high grades for that and high grades for picking a talent like Brenneman who would be threatening to most CEOs."

There was also serious work to do repairing Continental's ragtag image. To the public, and particularly, to frequent business fliers, nothing had changed. Continental looked like the same old carrier, with shabby-looking planes, a tacky orange and yellow color scheme, a dated logo and tired uniforms that made its employees look like ushers in an old movie theater.

"The old Continental was not attracting the business traveler because they just didn't perceive the carrier as one that could deliver a professional, reliable, comfortable and safe experience," says Steve Lawrence, of Lippincott & Margulies, a global marketing firm that helped Continental reshape consumer perceptions of the airline.

As Brenneman puts it, for a number of years, "Continental had been full of talk and broken promises." This time, he says, "If we were talking about change, we'd have to look like the change."

Bethune wanted Continental's image to be dynamic, responsive, consistent and professional. Implementing that strategy involved a full-scale makeover: a new golden globe logo, new interiors, tailored navy blue uniforms, new everything, down to the napkins and menus in first class— and greatly improved customer service.

This kind of image makeover is not cheap. But as Bethune says, "You can't make any money just cutting costs. People will only take that so far. Like if you were to go buy food, and if the food isn't clean, you don't care what it costs—you don't want it.

"Some people, like Delta, think cheaper is better, and you'll get more people on your planes by cutting your costs. But they are cutting the value-added part of the company. It's the cheese on the pizza that they're taking off to make the pizza cheaper. Instead, what you want to do is take the back-office accounting staff from the pizza factory out—not the cheese. I mean, don't give up things customers value. It's almost like if they said, 'You need to lose ten percent of your weight.' And then they want to cut ten percent of your tongue and ten percent of your eyes. You'd say, 'Wait a minute. No, no, no, no. Just the fat! Just the fat!' "

As head of technical operations, repainting became George Mason's responsibility. "It was an edict," he says. "Gordon called me in his office. This was about the third, fourth week that I was here. And he said, 'We need to get this paint job done—get the new image. We've got to complete this. Get with your guys, come back, and give me a plan.' And this was interiors, too, and other items, seats and carpeting, which came from suppliers, and they had lead times. So, I come back, and this was the end of '94, I came back with this plan. And the plan, taking advantage of every maintenance opportunity, said it would take twelve to thirteen months.

"Well. Gordon looked at me, and he said, 'Get it done by July 1,' " he remembers. "And, of course, I know Gordon very, very well. And I said, 'Gordon, these are all the opportunities we have.'

"Then, he says, 'I guess you better get some more opportunities, because, goddammit, if it's not done by July 1, then I'll get somebody to get it done by July. And so, if those marketing guys aren't going to give you the airplanes, you just tell them I can find another marketing guy, too.'

"He had a sense of urgency, and he wanted me to instill that sense of urgency in those people that had to cooperate with us to get it done," he says. "The job got done by July 1."

New image and all, the recovery still took time. Continental lost $131.8 million in 1994, earned $225 million in 1995, but didn't begin to boom until 1996. By 1997, however, the company was firmly entrenched as one of the premier carriers in the country. Still, there was room for improvement; among large airlines, Continental has the greatest potential for increasing traffic at its hubs, according to Brian Harris, an analyst at Lehman Brothers. Its local traffic in and out of its Newark, Houston and Cleveland hubs, he said, averages just 7 percent of the population in those metropolitan areas, compared with an average of 12.6 percent for all large airlines at their hubs.

Bethune was facing other, nonoperational, pressures as well. Back in 1993, David Bonderman, a Continental board member, had put together an investor group called Air Partners, which took the airline out of bankruptcy by investing around $60 million. Bonderman and his group, who controlled 51 percent of the shareholder's voting rights, wanted to cash out their remaining shares, now worth $519 million. They came very close to selling Continental to Delta Air Lines. That deal foundered, according to the *Wall Street Journal,* because Delta was unable to recognize how committed Continental management had become to the welfare of its employees. In the end, Delta would not guarantee the jobs and seniority of Continental's people, and neither Bethune nor his board would risk destroying the airline one more time by screwing the rank and file.

The result was an eleventh-hour deal between Continental and Northwest Airlines, respectively the fifth- and fourth-largest airlines in the country. The two companies are calling it a "joint venture," not a merger. Northwest bought a 14 percent stake in Continental, and the two will connect their global route systems, join their frequent flier programs and, in general, make it possible for passengers to deal with both airlines as if they were a single company.

Bethune predicts the joint venture will add a minimum of $500 million in revenue over the next three years, as each airline feeds new passengers to its partner. "This is a case where two and two make five, or even six," he told *The New York Times.*

These are blissful, though busy, days for Bethune. Continental has about $1 billion in the bank, a $250 million revolving line of credit, thirty-seven straight months of profits, as of May 1998, and is the dominant market presence in Houston, Newark and Cleveland. "You can run down the world's economy as much as you want, but we'll still be here," Bethune says. "We are consistently performing at the top of the industry. We have learned how to make this place work as a team." Bethune himself earned more than $20 million in 1996, thanks to performance-based stock options, and he's being touted in magazine after magazine as one of corporate America's most charismatic turnaround artists.

Looking back, Bethune says, "Every job I ever took was out of the blue—somebody called me up and said, 'Hey, would you consider doing this?' I never set any goals for myself, except to do a good job." And the secret to doing that? "The secret of success is simple," he says. "It's the ability to get people focused and working as a team. When I first started out as a mechanic, the goal was to find out what was wrong with the plane and fix it. But when I became a manager, I had to get fifteen people to work together to fix the plane, and that's not quite the same thing.

"You also have to have the strength to persevere in defining the right thing to do, and people have to believe in you—that takes credibility, sincerity and the ability to execute.

"Being a successful leader is like being a deer hunter," he says, adding that he has never actually shot a deer. "In a real good year, anyone can go out and shoot a deer. But in a bad year, you got to be a good shot. In other words, you have to be lucky, and you have to be ready. I have been at the right place at the right time but I was also ready. I had the skills. I didn't leave the shells at home."

3/Eckhard Pfeiffer
Racing Moore's Law

In October 1991, the headquarters of Compaq Computer Corp. looked as if it had been hit by disaster and was now in stunned mourning. News helicopters hovered over the headquarters north of Houston and reporters set up shop on-site. Meanwhile, throughout the campus employees clustered together in shell-shocked little groups, many wearing black armbands. Some simply went home, unable to work.

The cause of this communal catatonia was neither domestic terrorism nor some lethal viral outbreak. Rather, Rod Canion, the founder, CEO and driving force of the company, was gone. Fired. And his replacement, though long a part of the company, was barely known to most of the people around him.

Eckhard Pfeiffer was the new CEO, and he was stunned by what he saw. "The shock effect of what happened here was immense," he recalls. "There was almost paralysis over the campus, and I realized what monumental change had occurred and how it had impacted the people and the organization. That sank in the first hours of my being the CEO. Not only [was there] a feeling of not understanding, a feeling of loss, a feeling of confusion. There was also the question of why and what now? If this is so wrong—everything we've done—that they fired [Canion], then what's right?

"We immediately invited the top two hundred managers to the auditorium and communicated the event, something of the background and something of what we intended to happen. It was a very, very difficult meeting. It was quiet. There were people with tears in their eyes. And it sank in that total responsibility now is on my shoulders. You're expected to deliver. To set the right priorities and then get it going very quickly. I had to keep a clear mind and a clear thought in prioritizing what had to be done first to remobilize this entire company." It was a moment he had spent a career preparing for.

All revolutions eat their children. The computer revolution just does it faster. Who remembers Altair, Commodore, Zeos, Northgate? Virtually every major computer maker has had its near-death experience, including Dell and IBM, not to mention Apple or Wang or Digital or AST or Unisys. Then there's Compaq.

The Compaq Computer Corporation was born in a Houston pie shop, where three engineering refugees from Texas Instruments, Inc., Rod Canion, Bill Murto and Jim Harris, were drinking coffee. They had considered starting a chain of Mexican restaurants, but the allure of burritos and chiles rellenos quickly paled. Next, the jobless trio came up with the idea of an add-on hard drive for IBM's new personal computer, which had just been introduced in 1981 and was effectively creating the PC market.

They took their idea to the legendary venture capitalists Ben Rosen and L J Sevin in New York, but Rosen rejected their proposal. Instead, he made a counterproposal: Design an IBM-compatible portable computer. At the time it must have seemed as much a technological challenge as a potential business enterprise. The threesome returned to Houston and there, sitting in that now-famous pie shop, Canion sketched out his vision of Rosen's idea on the back of a placemat. Rosen and Sevin put up $2 million in venture capital, and in 1982, the world's first portable, IBM-compatible personal computer, a twenty-eight-pound hunk of innovation, came to market. It was a sensation. Compaq hit $1 billion in sales, won a listing on the New York Stock Exchange and landed a spot on *Fortune* magazine's list of the fifty largest U.S. industrial companies, all in less time than any other firm in U.S. industrial history.

And then it nearly died.

The computer industry waltzes to the merry tune of Moore's Law, named for Gordon Moore, a founder of Intel Corporation. In 1965, Moore predicted that the power of the computer chip would double every eighteen months, while the price dropped in half. He was right. A 1998 mid-line Compaq laptop that costs $1,500 delivers the computing power of a machine that would have cost tens of millions of dollars thirty years ago—not that such a machine could have been built. If the auto industry had changed at the same rate since 1960, a new midsized Ford might cruise at 400,000 mph and cost three cents.

Which brings us to a paradox. Here, at the center of this maelstrom, is fifty-seven-year-old Eckhard Pfeiffer, a methodical German famous for his remarkable ability to sit still and think. His friend and compatriot Andreas Barth, the German-born chief of Compaq's European operations, admiringly says, "He has *unglaubliche Geduld,* amazing patience." Pfeiffer oversees a management team of twelve executives—his direct reports—who weekly file into the Compaq boardroom on the company campus northwest of Houston. The meetings begin at 8 A.M. Tuesday mornings and often last all day, as this small group works, hour after hour, through the operational (mornings) and strategic (afternoons) questions that will determine the future of a $40 billion global technology leviathan.

Pfeiffer patiently and politely looks for flaws, lapses in logic, for the objective truth that he believes can be gleaned from his managers' testimony. He listens very carefully, smiles and waits a beat, asks another question.

It's all so methodical, so controlled and purposeful, that an onlooker tends to assume that this small group, who run possibly the most successful computer company of the 1990s, will infallibly choose the route to yet greater success. In 1997, Compaq sold in excess of ten million computers, more than any other company in the world. It controls 30 percent or more of the booming server market (servers are relatively powerful personal computers that enable other PCs to talk to each other in networks), and through its recent tandem acquisition, plays a part in most long-distance phone, fax and data line communications. Ten thousand dollars invested in Compaq stock in late 1991, when Pfeiffer took over, would be worth $140,000 at the close of 1997.

It's difficult to imagine that in the fall of 1991, the company announced its first losing quarter in history, laid off 12 percent of its workforce and was near collapse. When Pfeiffer was called in, it was not to preside over success, but to forestall disaster.

In 1964, Eckhard Pfeiffer, an ambitious young purchasing agent for Germany's giant electronics and telecommunications company, Telefunken, walked into the Geneva offices of an American firm called Texas Instruments, which was just inserting a toe into the European market. TI was a pioneer in semiconductors, the frontier technology of the day, and displayed a Texas wildcatter blend of ambition, bluster and optimism.

Pfeiffer had come to look at TI components, but he walked out with a job offer. Telefunken, he saw, "was a vast bureaucracy, and you could see how long it would take to reach a position of broad responsibility." Pfeiffer wanted a shorter road to power. This was it.

"I was only twenty-four, but they offered me a chance

to establish the business in Germany: find the offices, hire the staff, organize import and export of product. I hired the administrative staff, organized the accounting, the import and export of product, everything." In a few months, he had an efficient German company up and running. But TI was not a German company. Texas Instruments wanted growth and it wanted market share. This meant selling, and Pfeiffer, stiff, formal and serious, reverenced bureaucratic authority and would always respectfully take no for an answer. Salesmen don't work that way in Texas.

By contrast, Charlie Clough, Pfeiffer's newly appointed boss at TI's Geneva office, could sell anything. But he knew no German, nothing about German industry, and could barely find his way around the country. "TI sent me up there to build up enough of a customer base so that we could build a manufacturing plant in two or three years," Clough says, "but I couldn't even find the customers' offices."

Shortly after his arrival in Europe, Clough came to Stuttgart to introduce himself and to tell everyone how TI would sell its products in Germany. He spoke first to the three newly hired salesmen, then turned to Pfeiffer and said, "Who are you? What do you do?"

Pfeiffer recalls answering, "Well, Mr. Clough, I organized everything. I found the offices, bought the equipment, hired the staff and so on." To all of which, Clough responded, "This is nonsense. We've just lost a man in Hannover and you should be out selling. I'll give you a raise." (He doubled Pfeiffer's salary the next day.)

Pfeiffer protested the instantaneous rewriting of his job

description: "I've never made a sales call," he said. "You need formal training to be a salesman."

"Not at TI," Clough replied. "Don't worry, I never had any training. I tell you what, we'll travel together."

The next day, this Mutt and Jeff duo dropped in on Nordmende, a major German television manufacturer.

"When the head of purchasing found out we were not yet qualified by the technical people, he almost threw us out, but Charlie refused to leave," Pfeiffer recalls. "He kept saying, 'You must need something,' and he would flip the pages of the catalog." Clough eventually hit on item 213702 (Pfeiffer still remembers the product number), a tiny plastic transistor for televisions, which was cheap to produce and hugely profitable. "You must need these," he said.

The poor executive had never been the object of American-style salesmanship before. In Germany, you didn't enter a company's offices uninvited, and you always took "no" for an answer. Clough, to the visible discomfort of the Nordmende representative, did no such thing. And when he finally relented and agreed to test a few thousand TI transistors, Clough, to Pfeiffer's horror, exploded. "Are you crazy?" he hollered. "These are in such short supply that I couldn't possibly take such a small order. I have to have at least 300,000." After more haggling, the two went dancing down the stairs with an order in hand for 200,000. "I was ecstatic," Pfeiffer says.

Charlie Clough likes to say that the two of them went off in Pfeiffer's car on cold calls, searching through the phone book and dropping off samples at any organization with an electronic sounding name. "Half the places we called on were churches," he says with a laugh. Pfeiffer insists, also with a laugh, that none of this is true, but Charlie, he says with affectionate amazement, never let that get in the way of a good story.

A couple of years later, Pfeiffer and Clough had lunch with a former bicycle shop owner named Heinz Nixdorf at the Hannover Fair, a large annual industrial exposition. Nixdorf had designed a new transistorized computer, which he wanted to manufacture. The two salesmen were eager to close the deal, but this time it was Eckhard Pfeiffer, the one with the starched shirt, who took the lead. He scribbled out contract terms on a lunch menu and Nixdorf signed it. The menu-contract, which gave TI the job of producing the machine's integrated circuits, went off to Dallas, and Nixdorf's machines launched the German computer industry.

A series of successes followed, always higher on the TI ladder. According to several people who worked with him at the time, Pfeiffer proved himself a careful, controlled, prepared and relentless executive. As a high schooler, he had been a fiercely competitive tennis and soccer player. As an adult, he refused to fail, recalls Walden C. Rhines, the CEO of Mentor Graphics, who worked with Pfeiffer at TI. Rhines once told a reporter, "I never saw Eckhard miss a forecast. He'd sell the electricity out of the building before he'd miss a forecast."

In addition, Pfeiffer hired well because he took hiring very seriously and always did his due diligence. "That's how he found his wife," says Charlie Clough. "He was so careful in selecting the right person to become his secretary that he married her." Gary Stimac, who recently retired as a senior vice president in charge of Compaq's huge server division, recalls that Pfeiffer, from his first days with the company, "consistently hired people who were more capable than the job at hand might require, because he recognized that in three or four years he would need them if his part of the business grew as fast as he expected."

In 1980, at thirty-nine, Pfeiffer's work running TI's European consumer business caught the eye of company president Fred Buzy. A few months later, Buzy named him vice president in charge of corporate marketing. "It was a huge jump in scale," says Pfeiffer. "By then we had our own retail stores, and we had a huge distribution business in the States, plus the job included most of the marketing operations in Asia and Australia. All in all, it was a $500 million business."

But it was a troubled business, at a troubled company. TI had enjoyed thirty years of spectacular success as an *engineering* company. The mission was to design superb semiconductors and other electronic components, supported by what might be called the "Field of Dreams" marketing plan: If we build them they will come and buy them. This was well enough so long as the computer market was dominated by large business and scientific users. But, shades of Moore's law, as advances in technology pushed the semiconductor deeper and deeper into consumer markets, a different marketing model was needed.

This was true even if your technology was cutting edge, as was the case with TI, which had a 16-bit microprocessor long before anyone else. They had the opportunity to create the industry standard, as Intel was later to do, but the company failed to get their chip designed into products, into the marketplace. As Pfeiffer puts it, "Today we call it evangelizing, the whole business of generating interest, software programming, applications, sales incentives and so on. It's very complicated, time-consuming and expensive. But you have to do it to get your technology accepted and adopted. TI didn't understand this. For example, they spent a huge sum of money, maybe fifty million dollars, developing the 9900 microprocessor, but they wouldn't allocate the funds to go out and do the marketing."

Later, again badly misreading the market, TI began building its own PCs, but made them incompatible with the emerging IBM standard, basically ensuring their long-term failure.

As the company floundered, and TI's share of the world's integrated circuit market plummeted, CEO Mark Shepherd appeared to those around him to accept only the news he wanted. "When that happens, your department and division managers lose their own commitment, their identity, their self-confidence," Pfeiffer says. "They start to tell you what they think you want to hear rather than what you need to know." Shepherd began a chaotic series of reorganizations. Managers were reassigned and dismissed. One of Pfeiffer's colleagues from that time recalls "We had quarterly management meetings that could have been held in the Roman Coliseum. One manager became so nervous before his presentation that he lost his ability to speak."

"A large exodus of managers had begun early in 1983, and there was clearly going to be trouble for a long time to come," Pfeiffer says. "I began looking for other opportunities." He very nearly accepted the CEO job at a German-

American semiconductor manufacturer, then decided to work with a venture capitalist friend, test-marketing a company that would build the European operations of U.S. technology start-ups.

The first potential client they called on was the meteoric Compaq Corp., where Pfeiffer presented a detailed plan for setting up Compaq in Europe. The Compaq founders declined to relinquish control of their European future; instead, Canion asked Pfeiffer to join the company and do for it as an insider what he had just proposed doing as an independent contractor.

Pfeiffer declined, but Ben Rosen strongly supported Canion's choice of a European operations chief, and after a series of conversations over six weeks, Pfeiffer accepted the job, contingent on being released from his non-compete contract with TI.

In September 1983, one month after having left TI, and with a check from Canion for $20,000, Pfeiffer was on his way to Munich as vice president for Europe.

■

The Information Age was just dawning on the Continent. In the United States, after the 1981 launch of the IBM PC, the market for personal computers simply exploded. A whole raft of companies sprang into being, each making PC compatible machines, but still demand outstripped supply. In Europe, however, the acceptance of these new machines was slower, more cautious. "If IBM had focused on us for just a brief moment they could have crushed us before we ever got started," Pfeiffer says now. "They didn't bother."

Pfeiffer quickly set up wholly owned Compaq subsidiaries in Munich and London. By March, he had hired management and sales teams, signed up dealers and begun distribution. The British operation turned a profit in the first month, and he added a French subsidiary headquartered in Paris in 1984, while expanding into smaller European markets through authorized dealers.

Six years later, Pfeiffer was selling more computers abroad than the company was at home and had built his first factory, in Scotland, to insulate his operation from the effects of a strong U.S. dollar, which made buying his components from Compaq U.S. prohibitively expensive.

Gary Stimac recalls that when Pfeiffer was sent off to Europe, those in Houston who knew, hardly cared. "Our attitude among the senior management about Eckhard was, 'If Europe happens, it happens,'" he recalls. "Like most companies in our industry, we were following the IBM model. We thought our job was just to grow as fast as we could, and since America was the biggest market we were going to concentrate our efforts here. At the beginning, we used to hear about what Eckhard was doing, but we didn't pay much attention. Our focus was eighty percent inward."

Pfeiffer, once he had his operation up and running, hired with his usual care, keeping his head count low, which had the effect of keeping per-employee productivity and profit margins high. (As of 1997, Compaq achieved sales of roughly $1 million per employee, an astounding figure and the highest in the industry.) Having established Compaq in the major European markets, he moved on to all the smaller ones, then on to the Middle East, Africa and then Asia. By 1990, seven years after leaving Texas with that $20,000 check, Pfeiffer's overseas subsidiaries represented half the company's sales of $3.6 billion, and more than half the profits.

It didn't hurt that he and his people were working for a company that seemed to epitomize American innovation and enterprise. As Pfeiffer recalls those days, "The Compaq culture was unique. It was established very early on through the behavior—and lots of talk—by the founders, who all came from TI. They came from a situation that was troubling to them, where there was a lack of faith and loss of confidence in the management of the company. It caused the founders [of Compaq] to leave, and droves of people followed them. They said, one thing we don't want to be is what we just went through. We want to be happy to go to work every morning. We want a spirit of openness, trust, teamwork, to flow freely. That is the most constructive and creative environment. That's when people give their best." Compaq led by consensus, not by intimidation, Pfeiffer says.

Instead of adding another megalithic headquarters to the booming Houston skyline, Canion chose a pine-forested tract thirty miles outside of town, where he built a relaxed, West Coast–style campus. Every person occupied similar offices with similar furniture and equal access to sunlight. There was no reserved parking space for the CEO or anybody else. Employees enjoyed generous stock option and benefit plans, and at semiannual meetings, any employee could ask any question of any senior manager. Thousands turned out every time. They loved the culture Rod Canion built.

Throughout the 1980s, Canion's commitment to engineering excellence served as the horse that pulled the rest of the company along. Intel early on adopted Compaq as a testing ground for each of its PC processors, first the 8086, then the succeeding generations, the 286, the 386 and so on. This meant that by the time Intel was ready to release its next generation microprocessor to the industry as a whole, Compaq had already had a chance to design systems that could take advantage of it. That, in turn, allowed the company to maintain its technical edge in the marketplace. For example, Compaq released its first machine based upon Intel's 386 chip in 1986, almost a full year ahead of IBM.

The serpent in this paradise was, in a sense, the computer industry itself—the tiger desperately hanging on to the wagging tail of Moore's Law. "The computer industry moves so fast that you don't know about disaster until it has already happened," says Compaq chairman Ben Rosen. "We were out of touch with a market that no longer cared about brand name or retail service. What customers wanted was a reliable machine at a very competitive price, and our structure could not deliver that." Canion had no intention of delivering such a machine anytime soon. He thought he had time. He was wrong.

Throughout the 1980s the young computer industry was plagued by inconsistent quality. Many machines, using second-rate components, worked poorly or not at all, and the result was that buyers looked to make safe bets—even though the most trusted brands cost more money. This was a perfect situation for Compaq, whose mission was to build high-end, high-performance products, a strategy that kept profit margins high and in turn allowed Canion to invest continuously on research, quality control and the next generation of technology.

As the industry matured, however, quality improved across the board and by the end of the decade businesses and individual consumers were beginning to realize that they could buy with confidence from almost any computer manufacturer. Simultaneously, a host of companies realized that they could assemble excellent machines from off-the-shelf components, incurring no R&D costs, a saving that translated into lower and lower prices.

At Compaq, though, Canion's engineers remained focused on staying at the leading edge, ignoring the ever-broadening spectrum of the PC market, especially the low end. True, you could drop a Compaq on the floor without damage. But Dell made machines just as powerful, and you could buy two Dells instead of a Compaq, throw one out the window and you'd still save money. By the beginning of the 1990s, sales were falling, and inventories were rising.

"When the board asked what was going wrong, Canion blamed the recession," says Ben Rosen, Compaq's chairman of the board. "He insisted sales would come back when the economy picked up." From Europe, Pfeiffer argued that the problem wasn't recession, it was competition. Companies like Dell, AST Research, Zeos, Micron and Gateway 2000 were matching Compaq's quality at a fraction of the price. Pfeiffer had other concerns, as well. "We had grown just as fast in the international business as the company had in North America, but staff outside of the U.S. had remained very small. In Houston the head count had ballooned, and just as sales and profits were starting to fall, they were forecasting additional huge increases in staff."

Canion repeatedly assured his board and even his own staff that the market would return for Compaq's pricey machines and that a low-end model would eventually make its way to market, but not for a year or more, because it would take that long to develop the components. "It is better to leave the company in limbo for a time than to head off in the wrong direction," Canion insisted in a statement.

Limbo was just a little too close to hell for Rosen's taste. By the end of the summer of 1991, Compaq computers were becoming obsolete, sales were dropping precipitously, the company was about to report a first-ever quarterly loss of $70 million, and the stock price had fallen by more than two-thirds. Canion agreed to the company's first-ever layoffs, 12 percent of its workforce, some 1,400 people. Under pressure from his board to control costs, Canion brought Pfeiffer to Houston as executive vice president and chief operating officer, placing him just one rung below the pinnacle of power at the company. Still, neither Pfeiffer nor even Rosen, a veteran of many boardroom endgames, had any idea of the speed with which the corporate drama that followed would unfold.

As *The Wall Street Journal* later reported the tale, Rosen, prodded by a chance encounter with a junior-level Compaq employee, put together a small, secret internal team to show Canion that any competent computer engineer could build a computer with quality components in a matter of weeks, and for a fraction of the cost of a Compaq.

At the fall COMDEX computer show in Las Vegas, two members of the secret team, posing as entrepreneurs with an idea for a start-up, wandered the booths, buying clone components. They put together a working machine in their motel room in just three days, and in preparation for the next Compaq board meeting, the team assembled two working demonstration models.

On Thursday, October 24, the nine directors settled into their leather chairs around the U-shaped table in the windowless boardroom at the Compaq campus. Aware of Pfeiffer's internal campaign to speed a low-end model to market, Rosen had invited him to his hotel room at Houston's Ritz Carlton to view the demos. No one else knew what was to come.

For fifteen hours, Rosen and Canion, friends and builders of a remarkable organization, argued about Compaq's future. Finally, the soft-spoken Rosen delivered an ultimatum: Launch a low-cost machine within three months. "You could not build such a machine in that time frame, not without sacrificing the quality control and engineering excellence that Compaq represents," Canion replied.

"Yes, you could," said Rosen, and he lifted one of his demos onto the board table. "I did it with two of our people in only three days."

Still Canion would not bend, so the board offered him the face-saving option of resigning as CEO and taking a seat on the board. When he rejected their offer, they fired him. Before the board adjourned, Eckhard Pfeiffer was the new chief executive of Compaq. "To say we had confidence in Eckhard's ability to turn things around would not be a strong enough endorsement," Rosen says.

■

After that, all hell broke loose. Pfeiffer recalls that, in the early morning hours of the next day, he and a small group of advisors tried to figure out a way to get the news out to Compaq's employees. "We knew that while people were driving to work they would hear [about Canion's firing] on the morning news."

Pfeiffer's rebuilding task was complicated by the departure of half the senior management team over the next few days, including one of the founders. Part of the exodus was surely motivated by loyalty to Canion. But the real problem was that, for those who had helped to build the company, the prospect of wrenching change was simply too much. The head of worldwide manufacturing, for example, believed he was the lowest-cost producer on this globe until disabused by Pfeiffer, who made it clear that every element of the manufacturing process would have to change. The man, more in sorrow than anger, said that he had lived out his dream already, and couldn't face realizing a new one. The result: Pfeiffer had to field a senior team of new players, who were not, he says, "prepared."

To make matters still more difficult, Compaq had only two weeks before it had to face a financial analysts meeting, scheduled long in advance, for which every analyst of note had been invited to Houston. With Canion's firing the meeting suddenly became *the* place to be. Registration shot up and, says Pfeiffer, "I knew if I didn't deliver something on that day we would really be written off."

■

The situation was about as close to chaos as a corporation can get. For Pfeiffer, however, it is likely that nothing so trivial as corporate upheaval could cause him to lose heart, or his head. He'd lived through worse.

Shortly before he was born in Silesia in 1941, World War II had begun. His father was drafted into the German army and disappeared at the Russian front. As the German lines crumbled in 1944, Mrs. Pfeiffer and her children grabbed what they could carry and joined the stream of refugees pressing west. They walked hundreds of miles across Germany, to Bavaria.

"I remember," says Pfeiffer, with some reluctance. "Towards the end of the war, the planes were coming and you were told, 'As soon as you hear these things, throw yourself into the nearest ditch or hide behind something.' As soon as the war was over, there were other things, postwar terror by hordes of soldiers roaming around. And my father was a POW in Russia. [We didn't] know when or if he would come back."

Eckhard Pfeiffer was four years old when the war ended in 1945. "I remember streams of homeless people with no way to support themselves. My mother traded the last pieces of her jewelry for food. The authorities ordered those whose homes had survived the fighting to take in the homeless [and] we were placed with a farm family in a village of sixteen houses in the Bavarian countryside." The house was barely big enough for the owner's own family, but the Pfeiffers moved in alongside them. "You can imagine the feelings in this tiny village with its inbred culture," Pfeiffer says. "The owner of the house resented being forced to shelter these strangers. We were all so close together. There wasn't much food, mostly just what we could raise from these tiny plots of land that we were allocated, and there was no work, no jobs, no money."

The experience, he says today, "left a very strong will to—I don't want to exaggerate and say survive—but somebody had to bring the bread and something to the table. It was available—we lived in a small village with farmers all around, so there was bread, eggs and meat. But it didn't belong to us, so it had to be gained somehow.

"My early childhood created certain beliefs and certain objectives, you might almost say. When I had to do something I had to do it. And when I had to ask for something I had to ask for it. I did what it took to get the job done. So you're left with this anxiety. So you know the cost of disorder."

To restore order, Pfeiffer had two constituencies to placate: his own people and the financial community. And with his company hemorrhaging money and brand equity, he had to do it fast. What he did was utterly characteristic. He went home and thought through the problem. "We were a company that was very good at what it was doing in a particular segment, and that segment was under attack and we weren't ready for it. The market conditions had changed, customer needs and demands had changed and we had not responded.

"I spent two full days just going through specifics. I worked on it very intensely. Prior to that it was just fragments: Why aren't we doing this, or why did we keep resisting such and such, or why are we not dealing with the market demand or that customer complaint. Where is it going?"

Pfeiffer's analysis was as follows: Compaq had great design and manufacturing strengths, with an extraordinary core of 1,200 engineers, and an unexcelled reputation for quality and reliability. But computers were becoming a commodity, which meant the critical variable was price. The task, then, was for Compaq to transform itself into the low-cost designer, the low-cost manufacturer, while protecting the reputation of the brand.

Pfeiffer had also learned, from his years at TI, the importance of market share. "TI was fiercely focused on market share [because of] the price-learning curve principle: With every doubling of volume you're cutting your cost in half," he says. "It was one of these semiconductor phenomena," he adds wryly. The upshot was that he felt his company could rapidly gain market share from its competitors, if it could overhaul its pricing, product line and marketing.

"The vision and the strategy [was that] Compaq will continue to serve the high performance segment, but in addition we'll compete right at the entry level and all the way up, covering the entire product spectrum. We'll cover every market segment; including the difficult ones, like the school market, the government market and the consumer market, which would be the ultimate test in whether we could be that new efficient company."

Pfeiffer came back to work on Monday, "clear," to use a word he favors, about what his company should do. That week, he crafted an address of quite remarkable directness and urgency to the analysts who began flocking to Houston. Compaq was "in the midst of a marketing revolution," he told them, one which had "galvanized our entire corporation" and would transform it. At the same time, he announced a new team of senior managers to help him carry out his plans. Wall Street was impressed enough to wait and see if he could deliver.

Next came his own people. While it was true that Pfeiffer was galvanized, everybody else was confused. "It took a long time [for my plan] to sink in," he says today. "There were senior managers on the team who six months later, nine months later, said to me, 'In all honesty, look, I followed you, but I didn't understand what would happen.' They did not see the breadth of the actions and initiatives and how it would ultimately all fit together."

According to one journalist who has covered Compaq since the early days, "One thing I know that [Pfeiffer] did that I don't think was ever done before is he started these regular meetings of all the top managers of the company. And he really told them everything; it was a real out-and-out exchange of ideas. He told them how urgent matters were and some of them were not afraid to tell him what needed to change."

Management Communications meetings traditionally had been held once a quarter, if that often; that had to change. "It was difficult because there was no relationship,

not a grown trusted long-lasting relationship," Pfeiffer recalls. " 'What's he saying?' they asked themselves. 'Is it
something we can build a future on—our hopes, our careers?' Communication was really at a premium, so at the
very early stages we had two meetings a week, then one,
for two months, through Christmas of 1991.

"In this very early stage there was this huge question
mark: Will he maintain the Compaq culture? I kept hearing
this: I had our PR and HR people try to find out what were
the main issues for people, and it was the culture, the culture, the culture."

This went on for some weeks, the managers worrying
and Pfeiffer reassuring, until Pfeiffer simply got fed up and
confronted the issue directly. "I got mad," he says. Perhaps,
but in his characteristically analytical manner. Pfeiffer
didn't threaten and he didn't bluster. Rather, he stood up at
yet one more Communications meeting and cut straight to
the logical heart of the issue. "Let me tell you something,"
he said. "I have been with this company since 1983, longer
than most of you here. I have grown over half this company's business and any one of you who has ever visited
one of these countries where we operate today, tell me now
where you have not found the Compaq culture. And then
ask yourselves who opened these subsidiaries, who hired
the country manager, who got it all going?" It was a devas-
tating salvo, and it blew the culture question away.

Still, Pfeiffer understood that corporate cultures neither
survive nor thrive on discussion alone. The company has to
walk its talk, making its words credible in the marketplace.
So, the day Pfeiffer became CEO, he told an on-line industry newsletter that his engineers would at once begin de-

signing a new line of PCs, "with a much more aggressive pricing position." Compaq had always been an engineering company, and engineering is a secular religion of sorts, a contemplative calling. But Pfeiffer was a marketer, and marketing is essentially the commercial practice of total war. Pfeiffer, in effect, told his troops that Compaq's competitors were the enemy and that he was bent on overrunning them.

To that end, he immediately began raising the number of dealers carrying Compaq products, which quintupled over the next two years—from 3,000 to 25,000. He cut prices 30 percent to 50 percent across the board, setting off a price war that, over the next couple of years, killed off many of Compaq's more fragile competitors.

In addition, hundreds of employees were reassigned to customer service and support, expanding that operation by 50 percent. In this regard, says Gary Stimac, "Eckhard was [always] different. He focused on customers. He'd deliver products by taxicab if that made customers happy. We treated customers like dogs and gave them what we wanted them to eat. Eckhard tried to find out instead what the dogs wanted." Pfeiffer also fired Compaq's ad agency, determined to create a completely new corporate image.

This push began to increase sales almost at once. And in January, with the company beginning to gather momentum, Pfeiffer announced that, from here on out, Compaq would not be underpriced by any manufacturer, anywhere in the world. "After that," said Ross Cooley, then head of North American operations, "none of us looked back."

In June 1992, just nine months after Pfeiffer took over, he announced forty-one new products, this at a company whose former CEO had boasted shortly before his dismissal of releasing nine new products in an entire year. Pfeiffer declared Compaq a "relaunched" company, and in a twelve-page insert placed in magazines and newspaper to coincide with the new product debuts, told everyone who would listen: "We have a new mission. A new goal . . . products that are exactly what you need, easy to find and priced right."

The new computers included the ProLinea line, which was Compaq's first true consumer product. It cost under $1,000 and the reviewers declared it a quality product—a real Compaq. It quickly became the hottest-selling machine in the country.

Between the new machines and the price cuts on the old ones, shipments rose 40 percent in the third quarter of 1992, while revenues soared 50 percent. Overall profit margins declined sharply, from 43 percent the last healthy year under Canion to 29 percent, but as Pfeiffer had predicted, volume grew so fast that unit costs fell. In fact, in 1993, as volume doubled to three million computers, manufacturing costs actually fell nearly $10 million. The stock soared, and market share by the end of 1994 had risen from 3.5 percent to 10 percent. Compaq became, "One of the great turnarounds in the world," Credit Suisse/First Boston Corp. analyst Charles Wolfe told *Business Week.*

Pfeiffer made nearly as big an impact killing a project he inherited as he had starting new ones. "We were all very envious of what Hewlett-Packard had accomplished with their printing business," says Rosen. "You might not be able to make very much on an individual printer, but you always had the consumables business, the cartridges and rollers and so on. And we had a strong brand name. Most people who bought a computer in those days also needed a printer, so why give that business to someone else? And since HP was beginning to make personal computers, why not try to do something to cut into their sixty percent market share in printers. It all sounded like a great business." Canion agreed and strongly backed the initiative in late 1989.

The rollout of the new printers finally came about in August 1992. Critics loved them. "Editor's Choice for High Speed Printing," sang *MacWorld*. "Best Buy for '93," said *Corporate Computing*. In the first thirty days, the printers garnered eleven top industry awards. But the business prospect wasn't nearly so rosy. As the first machines began reaching the stores, Pfeiffer could see the battle with Hewlett-Packard unfolding. "In a very tough economic environment, we were up against an overwhelming competitor. To make any headway, we would need a very large number of machines in place and an additional layer of people to provide the consumables. In the meantime, we would be pouring much more money into the business than we had budgeted." Pfeiffer had just eliminated 1,400 jobs. He wasn't about to expand the head count again to support a business he didn't have confidence in. "Besides," he says, "our core business, selling PCs, was coming back very strongly. I made a decision to get out."

Thanks to Compaq's partnerships with dozens of other companies, disposing of the business proved relatively painless. Xerox took over the patents, warranties, customer service, even the inventory. The manufacturing capacity was quickly absorbed by the rapidly expanding PC lines. The total write-off for the project came to something less than $50 million. On sales that year of $7.2 billion, that hardly counted as a rounding error.

"Compare it to New Coke or to the Edsel," says Ben Rosen. "It hardly counts." By failure standards, it was a great success, but for Pfeiffer the lesson was not so positive. "I hadn't been digging enough about what would follow," he says. "The initial product clearly had all the technical leadership attributes we wanted. What was not sufficiently well planned was the strategy for moving beyond the initial success. We had no road map, and no clear appreciation of the magnitude of the total investment required to enter an entirely new business."

Pfeiffer also felt that some of those working on the printer project had become so attached to it that they were building their business plans more on wishful thinking than on truly solid projections. "It's natural for people to want to protect a project they've worked on. But we have a culture of openness here, going back to Rod Canion's management ideas," says Pfeiffer. "When the errors are revealed in little doses, it damages everyone. Other people in the team are willing to help if you tell them the size of the problem, but if you keep it from them and then they get involved, it becomes their problem too. It is a big disappointment when people don't have the openness and maturity to lay out the difficulties."

The lesson for Compaq managers was, don't fudge; if you want to retain the culture, then lead with the truth.

After the June 15 product release, the atmosphere on campus seemed a bit less electric. Compaq was back on its feet. "There was this feeling of 'what next?' " says Pfeiffer. "It's [the rescue] done, it's moving, it's widely accepted. So what's the next goal. How do you keep people focused and excited?"

As usual, Pfeiffer thought about it. He saw that IBM was in serious trouble, and that Apple was beginning to experience difficulties. So he asked one of his market research people to put together all the possible trend lines tracking Compaq versus its competition. After studying previous and projected five-year trends, Pfeiffer told his senior people at a staff meeting that his new goal was to become number one in the global PC industry. It was déjà vu all over again, he says. "They all looked at me, really, like 'Now he has lost it. We are barely out of the hole and here he comes with another one of these ideas.' But very quickly it began settling in and they supported it, communicated it, and from then on every business plan was developed and focused on when we would become number one and what it would take. I set the most cautious goal of 1995."

Instead, Compaq leapfrogged IBM and Apple by the end of 1994, not 1995. They were number one.

Once again Pfeiffer responded by raising the bar. The new goal was to become the industry leader in customer satisfaction, an exercise that would force the company for the first time to define what that meant and devise metrics to measure it. It turned into a three-year project, involving company-wide assessments and biannual surveys. The pursuit of this goal, says Pfeiffer, "helped tell us where we are weak, where we are deficient, what we need to focus on, where the competition ahead of us is. It helps us to steer the ship."

This time, Pfeiffer preempted the problem of coming up with a new goal. In mid-1996, he says, Compaq completed a three-month "internal change analysis." "Coming off forty-five percent growth each year for five years, we said this is too dangerous. We're getting carried away with our own success. Let us attack it before we get attacked." His staff put together fifteen internal teams, each with roughly ten people and each tasked with analyzing every part of the business, from enterprise and desktop computers, to manufacturing, to distribution and marketing, to internal organization. The teams then came together to make their recommendations to the senior managers.

Based on their analyses Pfeiffer made a worldwide Compaq internal announcement, via video-conferencing and other means, on July 1, 1996. He unveiled an entirely new corporate direction and a new organization to match it. "Compaq the PC supplier would become Compaq the global computer company," he says. "This included extending our consumer division beyond the PC into everything that might appear in the evolving digital household, from 'smart' appliances to HDTV to Internet access."

To the astonishment of everybody, including Pfeiffer, the five-year projections of the change analysis teams showed that Compaq would be a $40 billion operation in 2000, an enormous increase from the $24.61 billion in sales for 1997 (and a mind-boggling leap from Compaq's $3.5 billion revenue in 1991, when Pfeiffer took over). Pfeiffer, in typical fashion, revised the number upward to $50 billion after he spent $3 billion in June 1997 to acquire Tandem Computers, which specializes in so-called enterprise critical operations such as those that keep stock markets trading, global fund transfers zipping around the world and 911 emergency services operating.

To Pfeiffer, that $50 billion figure meant one thing: a new goal. "The new battle cry was 'Number Two,' " he said. By the year 2000, he wanted Compaq to be not just the biggest PC manufacturer, but also the second biggest computer company in the world, period (he had started out as number sixteen). And he wasn't through.

On January 26, 1998, the computer world woke to still another Pfeiffer thunderbolt: Compaq had bought Digital Equipment Corp. (DEC) for $9.6 billion—the industry's biggest deal ever. Overnight, Compaq had become a $38 billion company. More important, it had leapt into what *The Economist* called "another league"—one in which Compaq no longer just made very good, very cheap PCs, but also had a blue-chip, 22,000-person-strong global service operation, which large corporations expect when they make their huge technology purchases. Finally, in acquiring DEC, Compaq for the first time had access to leading edge research and development.

Once again, the relentlessly competitive Pfeiffer had set a stretch goal for his company, then leapfrogged it—a process that, over his tenure as CEO, has created a Compaq culture that, while compatible with the old one, has a ferocious edge to it. *Fortune* magazine senior writer David Kirkpatrick, who has followed Pfeiffer for many years, says, "People work hard in technology, but I've never seen a company where they work harder than at Compaq. Compaq is a place where I would almost venture to say that the typical employee works harder that the typical Microsoft employee. Somehow Eckhard has instilled a culture in

Compaq, a desire to win, that is just phenomenally vivid in the minds of everyone who works there. It is close to a commodity industry, and yet they have succeeded in differentiating themselves well beyond what most people would have considered possible."

That culture, and Pfeiffer's leadership, will be tested more severely now than at any point since he took the helm. Growth in the PC market, Compaq's bread and butter, has been slowing, and as of mid-1998, only cross-state arch-rival Dell Computer is sustaining double-digit growth in sales and profits. Moreover, Dell, which sells directly to purchasers, not through stores, shares no revenue with middlemen and thus enjoys a 10 percent or so price advantage over Compaq. This is critical, because the increasing commodification of the PC means that, sooner or later, price and compelling brand marketing will become the only bases on which consumers make their purchasing decisions.

Then there is Digital—the masterstroke that Pfeiffer hopes will transform Compaq into a top-tier global computer manufacturer and service provider—on a par with Hewlett-Packard and IBM. Strategically, it is a sound move. But Pfeiffer intends to cut fifteen thousand Digital jobs, as well as two thousand at Compaq. Merging operations often causes massive layoffs—indeed, the economies they can realize are one reason for the mergers in the first place. But such actions may also wreak havoc on the morale of those remaining, cause others to seek work elsewhere, and in general sap the commitment, vitality and creativity needed to keep pace in the computer industry. Observers got a glimpse of the potential problems at Digital's June 1998 general shareholder meeting, during which several employees spoke bitterly of the merger and the coming layoffs.

As if that weren't enough, Pfeiffer is still faced with the task of integrating Tandem into his company. Not only does Tandem occupy a completely different niche in the computer market, but its founder and CEO quit within three months after he assumed overall responsibility for sales marketing at Compaq. This is arguably the second most important post in the company, and the most important strategic position, for as I mentioned, the *price* at which you can produce PCs and the efficiency with which you can *market* them, will ultimately decide who owns the PC market. Pfeiffer is a past master of the manufacturing side of the equation, but it remains an open question whether he will prove equally masterful at marketing.

Every morning, Eckhard Pfeiffer, the president and chief operating officer of Compaq Computer Corp., pulls onto the highway and heads for work at high speed, quickly pushing his beloved black Porsche into high gear. "In the morning, I see other faces, people just rolling along. There is not time in this job to just roll along. There is an intensity to it, a sense of urgency that comes partly from the nature of the industry. You have to pace yourself, keep a balance in your life, but you must keep your momentum. You must keep moving."

How long Pfeiffer will keep moving at this pace is anyone's guess, but thus far his appetite for the race remains undiminished. The fact that he still has competitors seems almost to affront him. Never mind the success of firms like Dell Computer and Gateway. Their time will come, he vows. Meanwhile, Tandem will, he says, project his company into the most complex and expensive computing applications, and he continues to push the price of his low-end machines down to unheard-of levels. (Early in 1998, a Presario with a Pentium chip could be had for under $800, monitor included.)

Chief strategist Bob Stearns remarked of Pfeiffer to a national business magazine early in 1996: "I've never met anybody more competitive and tenacious. He does not lose. And he's never satisfied. You cannot satisfy him." The race with Moore's Law never ends, however; it only increases in velocity. Pfeiffer has already worn out several sets of Compaq senior managers, and as the computer industry evolves and morphs in unpredictable, wrenching ways, the question is how long any man, however determined, can remain abreast of it.

4/Robert Eaton and Robert Lutz
The Copilots

What makes a leader? Bob Eaton, the chairman of
Chrysler Corp., has a succinct answer. "A leader
is someone who can take a group of people to a
place they don't want to go or to a place they don't think
they can go."

That definition might serve as well as a description of
Eaton's own performance at Chrysler, where he took the
helm in mid-1992 and announced to the world: "I want to
be the first chairman in the history of Chrysler not to lead
the company back from bankruptcy." That in itself was an
ambitious goal, given that the company he had been picked
to lead had been in and out of serious financial trouble

since 1925, when Walter Chrysler renamed for himself an ailing car company called Maxwell Motors.

In the event, Eaton proved as good as his word, posting sterling results quarter after quarter, and creating a design and management team that became the envy of the automobile industry. Still, in stark contrast to his predecessor, Lee Iacocca, Eaton remained as self-effacing as it was possible for the CEO of one of Detroit's Big Three carmakers to be. But that ended for good on May 6, 1998, when *The Wall Street Journal* broke the news that Chrysler and Daimler-Benz, the Stuttgart-based maker of Mercedes-Benz cars and trucks, were in merger talks. The article, headlined, "New World Order," was one of those rare business stories of genuine global significance: The car business is one of the primary engines of the world economy, it would be the largest industrial merger ever, and it would be the first ever merger between major German and American corporations. Finally, industry insiders were amazed that the two companies had kept their negotiations secret.

Just one day later, Eaton and Daimler-Benz chairman Jürgen Schrempp announced at a London press conference that the German industrial giant would acquire Chrysler in a deal worth roughly $92 billion, creating the third-largest auto and truck maker, after General Motors and Ford. Afterward, analysts confidently predicted that the deal would lead to massive global consolidation among carmakers. One commentator even said that the big news wasn't the merger itself, but what would happen in its wake. For his part, Eaton quickly found himself on nightly news shows on every continent, and on the front pages of every significant newspaper, newsmagazine and business magazine in every industrialized nation.

A few weeks later, Eaton sat in his office in Auburn Hills, Michigan, and reflected on what he had done, and why. The interview was vintage "Bob," as virtually everyone calls him. He spoke openly and thoughtfully, with the calm of a man who knows himself and his business, occasionally pausing to regard the misty landscape outside his window before resuming his conversation.

"Up until last summer [1997]," he said, "we really did feel we could go it alone and become the premier automobile company in the world." In July, however, Eaton gave a speech to an internal management meeting in which, he says, "I talked about the big things that were coming—in fact I used the book *The Perfect Storm* as an analogy [the book concerns an ocean storm produced by the optimal conditions for creating violent weather]. Three fronts approaching from different directions were likely to hit us at the same time and be the 'perfect storm' for this industry." Those fronts, he said, were a revolution in how cars are sold, a greater capacity to produce cars than there are consumers to buy them, and the overall competitiveness of the car market.

"The waves would be a hundred-foot, and we were going to be a sixty-foot boat," Eaton told his managers. He was convinced that a huge shakeout was on its way, and felt that the Asian economic collapse that was beginning toward the close of 1997 would only hasten it along.

Searching for ways to respond strategically to this future, and under cover of total secrecy, Chrysler and

Daimler-Benz had for eight months been studying the possibility of large-scale joint ventures. The biggest of these was called "Q-star," which would have merged the international operations of both corporations as a single company. Neither Q-star nor any of the other projects ever made it off the drawing board, however, a result that left Eaton conspicuously unperturbed. "Frankly, I've never been much on joint ventures," he says. "I've always had the philosophy that if you have two different management teams and two different markets, at any given time they can be aligned. But this is a long time-horizon industry and by the time you get your first product out there you can have management changes, et cetera, et cetera. So [joint ventures] don't work very well in this industry and never have."

The possibility of a merger never even came up for discussion during the eight months that Chrysler and Daimler-Benz people were closeted with each other. This was odd, not just because of subsequent events, but because, in Eaton's words, "I've said forever that mergers do work, because you end up with one management, one business plan, one compensation system."

Then, on January 12, 1998, Jürgen Schrempp came to Eaton's office and, in a fifteen-minute conversation, laid out his case for a merger. He found an extremely attentive audience. In fact, Eaton had been thinking along very similar lines, and negotiations moved swiftly after the CEOs reached their personal understanding on what they were trying to achieve. It was pretty straightforward, says Eaton: "We decided from day one that we were going to merge the companies; we were not going to have Daimler-Chrysler be a holding company." And the goal of this new entity? "To put together the premier, the number one transportation company in the world and at some point maybe even the number one company in the world, period."

From the very beginning, Eaton told his top four executives where he was headed. "I did not know what their response was going to be," he recalled, but "the response was overwhelmingly positive. And these were people like Thomas Stahlkamp, who had every reason to believe that when I left he would be the chairman. [Thomas T. Stahlkamp was picked in January 1998 to fill retiring Bob Lutz's slot as Chrysler president. Like Eaton, Stahlkamp is unpretentious, modest and self-effacing. "Why me? many of you have asked," he said to the dozens of reporters gathered at his post-promotion press conference. "I'm sure there are going to be days ahead when I ask myself that."] Then I brought the board in. Again, I assumed that I had their support, but I wasn't sure. And of course I did. As we brought people on I expected we would get some who were not very enthused—lukewarm at best and maybe absolutely opposed. It just didn't happen." Even the United Auto Workers union and its German counterpart supported the merger proposal, agreeing with Eaton that, ultimately, an even stronger automobile company would be the result.

Now Eaton is readying himself for his new job, as he waits for SEC approval of the merger. "My job is to integrate these two great companies into the premier transportation company in the world." It's a far, far cry from his situation back in March 1992, when Lee Iacocca announced that Robert Eaton would be his successor at the Chrysler Corporation. At the time, a lot of people in the car industry said, "Bob who?" Eaton had enjoyed a long and successful career at General Motors, where he had risen through the engineering ranks before being sent off to Zurich, Switzerland, as head of GM's extensive European operations. Still, he was hardly a high-profile figure in an industry filled with marquee names. And with that relative obscurity came another, more important question: "Bob why?"

Certainly, there was nothing in Eaton's career that would have suggested that he was the man of that particular hour for Chrysler. A quiet, almost shy Kansan, Eaton was most comfortable working on complex production problems. When he did appear in public, at events such as the huge North American International Auto Show in Detroit, he was usually alone, without the phalanx of General Motors public relations people who typically surround senior GM executives. At fifty-one, the ruddy, open-faced Eaton was the very antithesis of the charismatic Iacocca, and at the time of his appointment, Chrysler seemed dearly to need another shot of charisma.

As Eaton says, "Every time you picked up the paper, you were reading something bad about Chrysler. It seemed disorganized, lacking in product, and without the money to be a significant player in the car business."

Significantly, this view appeared to have been ratified by Wall Street in the autumn of 1991. As Chrysler sought to raise money to bring out its new car line, Philip Fricke, Prudential Securities's respected auto industry analyst, pulled Prudential out of its role as colead underwriter barely two weeks before the offering. Fricke doubted that the company could survive, and when Eaton assumed the chairmanship fifteen months later, Chrysler was not much better off.

In fact, between 1988 and 1992, Chrysler was, to all appearances, an unfolding disaster. Iacocca, who had run Chrysler from 1978 to 1992, saved the company from bankruptcy once and then drove it right back into deep trouble. When Iacocca came from Ford to take control of Chrysler, the company's products were wretchedly made, prone to rustout and breakdowns. The company was nearly bankrupt, and only a $1.5 billion Federal loan guarantee, coupled with a nearly $2 billion grab bag of concessions from the unions, dealers and parts suppliers, allowed Chrysler to bring out the series that would ultimately save it: the K-platform.

The K-cars were everything that Chrysler's previous offerings were not. They were low-priced, fuel-efficient, reliable and relatively well made. By 1985, Iacocca had passed through his self-described "five years of hell" and was riding high on the K-car's success. In 1983, Iacocca's Chrysler introduced two new K-car variations: the Dodge Caravan and Plymouth Voyager, America's first minivans. So thoroughly did the public embrace the low-cost, high profit, easy-to-build minivan, that within a few years of its introduction, the company was selling upward of half a million of them a year. Minivans brought the company back from the brink, allowing it to repay its federally guaranteed loans more than a decade ahead of schedule. A series of Chrysler television commercials starring Iacocca, followed by the introduction of the minivan, made Iacocca arguably the most famous businessman in the world, a status he built upon by writing an autobiography that sold eight million copies and by chairing the Statue of Liberty/Ellis Island Restoration committee. By 1988, he was being spoken of seriously as a potential presidential candidate.

But even as Iacocca enjoyed his success, the bill was coming due on a series of critical errors. First, in order to protect the company from the cyclical nature of the automobile business, he had made a number of substantial investments outside the automobile industry. In quick succession, he bought Gulfstream Aerospace, Electrospace Systems, Finance America, E. F. Hutton Credit and four car-rental firms. The acquisitions, plus a downturn in the auto market, rapidly shrank Chrysler's working capital, which fell from $14.3 billion in 1988 to $1.7 billion by the time Eaton became chairman in 1992. Ford and GM, too, had diversified their portfolios—GM bought Hughes Electronics and Ross Perot's EDS, for example—but the number one and number two carmakers were financially much stronger corporations, with capital reserves vastly larger than Chrysler's.

Second, with Chrysler's limited resources going to diversification, there was less money for new car designs, which are the competitive engine of an automobile company. As early as 1979, Iacocca had put the development of a new full-sized pickup truck on indefinite hold, and all through the 1980s, as the company's prospects improved, he resisted spending money on new car projects. Instead, he pushed Chrysler's engineers to develop increasing numbers of variants off the K-platform. Besides the van, there was a convertible, several midsized sedans, and an ungainly, narrow-wheelbased luxury sedan, the Chrysler Imperial.

Iacocca the celebrity was also becoming increasingly distant from the team of talented managers he had brought over with him from Ford—the so-called "Gang of Ford." The chairman liked the spotlight and he got it, often for the wrong reasons. A messy and well-publicized divorce, and at least one attempt to sell the company to Italy's Fiat, which ended in a public row with the patrician Fiat chairman, Gianni Agnelli, seriously undermined morale at Chrysler's headquarters in the Detroit enclave of Highland Park.

How bad was morale? An internal survey of workers and managers, quoted in Brock Yates's excellent book, *The Critical Path*, tells some of the story. One unnamed middle management executive put it this way: "Does Iacocca think his making $20 million a year and continually asking the rest of us to sacrifice is going to work forever?" And then–Chrysler president Harold Sperlich, who played a key role in developing the Ford Mustang and had come over to Chrysler just before Iacocca, later declared, "Lee Iacocca became Henry Ford [II], the very man he hated most."

With the company hemorrhaging money, Chrysler's board, which had been more than willing to indulge Iacocca's imperial style when he was selling the government bailout to Congress and later making money, now put together a multimillion-dollar package of incentives to ease him into retirement. It included a generous cash payout, over a hundred thousand shares of Chrysler stock (in addition to the millions of dollars in options he already had), use of the company jet and the purchase of Iacocca's homes in Boca Raton, Florida, and Bloomfield Hills, Michigan. He accepted the offer, though he made it clear that he wanted to wait until the 1993 model LH sedans—the Dodge Intrepid, Chrysler Concorde and Eagle Vision—were introduced before he would step aside.

Chrysler might have solved its succession problems easily, by elevating Robert Lutz, the incumbent president of Chrysler. Lutz was a widely respected "car guy," a Swiss-born former U.S. Marine aviator who loves fast motorcycles, faster cars, flies jet fighters for kicks and stirs cream into his coffee with a pocket knife, then licks the blade clean. He had spent much of his career in Europe, first with General Motors, then as head of sales at BMW, and finally as chairman of Ford of Europe. It was Lutz who had developed Chrysler's ultimate thrill machine, the muscular Dodge Viper, whose roadster lines, open cockpit and monster V-10 engine were unlike anything Detroit had ever produced. He followed that by championing the Chrysler's LH sedans, whose "cab forward" design raised the standard for roominess and passenger comfort in family cars. The LH cars, whose initials Detroit wags said stood for "last hope," along with the new Jeep Grand Cherokee, which had been in the works when Chrysler bought American Motors in 1987, brought Chrysler back from the brink. These were, according to Yates, "the opening salvo in Chrysler's new company-saving edition of vehicles."

Unfortunately for Lutz, Iacocca simply loathed the idea of sharing credit even for Chrysler's smaller successes, much less the larger ones. He also had come to distrust Lutz, who had very publicly opposed the Fiat merger. In any case, as Lutz began, in Yates's words, to "build his own company within the company, Iacocca was preparing to shoot him in the saddle. There was no doubt that he was privy to Lutz's increasingly sharp criticism of his stewardship and surely took umbrage." And so, at Iacocca's instigation, the company's board passed over Lutz at a time when Chrysler was truly in desperate straits.

Thus, even before Eaton actually arrived on the premises, he had a major problem: Lutz was widely expected to quit. Worse, if he didn't leave, the automotive press predicted Chrysler would divide into two warring camps, immobilized by loyalties to the two top managers.

In any event, all the insider analysis proved dead wrong. "I had talked to some people I knew in Europe, people I respected," says the square-jawed Lutz, "and they all told me the same thing. Bob Eaton was not your typical arrogant American executive. He knew how to listen before making up his mind. Then I talked to him myself. We had a series of dinners and I decided that this was the man who could take Chrysler into the next century." Lutz pauses, then adds, "It also helped that I had worked at most of the other major companies. I couldn't see myself going back to any of those places."

Lutz was also concerned by other matters, and other people, should Eaton fail. "There was all this talk about the board bringing in a complete outsider, somebody from outside the car business. I was very worried about somebody from outside the business who would come in and do a clean sweep. Bob Eaton's presence gave me a sense of relief."

Characteristically, Eaton plays down the whole idea of a potential conflict with Lutz. "Remember," he says, "I was being told by everyone that this company didn't have a chance to survive. Bob Lutz told me that I should take a close look around the company, and make up my own mind if it was true. When I did, I was very pleasantly surprised at just how good it had the potential to become. And finally, it was clear that Bob Lutz and the management of Chrysler had a plan for getting Chrysler moving."

It quickly became apparent that Eaton and Lutz, despite their vastly different backgrounds, shared a common worldview. Both had spent much of their careers getting their hands dirty—literally—tinkering with cars. Both had spent significant portions of their careers in Europe, away from Detroit's executive intrigues. And both knew how to inspire the loyalty of the engineering and production managers who are essential to making cars profitably, Lutz with his charismatic Marine personality, and Eaton because his engineering background assured other engineers that they were talking a common language. "I knew we'd click as a team," says Lutz.

For his part, Eaton was repeatedly surprised by the caliber of his new colleagues. "I thought the biggest challenge I would have would be to get a decent product program, to build a strong team," he says. "Everything that was in the media suggested that Chrysler was in total disarray. Well, after I signed the contract, I walked around the design studios and saw the cars that [Design Vice President] Tom Gale and his team were working on, and I was just blown away. And while the team we have here wasn't in leadership positions for the most part, they were here, working at Chrysler. We didn't have to go out and hire a terrific team, we just had to lead them differently. We've changed very few people near or at the top, whereas our competitors over the past five years have made some significant changes. We had good people. We didn't have to hire any-body from the outside."

Eaton, a genuinely modest man, well liked even within Detroit's inbred, backbiting car community, invariably points to others when prodded to speak of his achievements. He has an instinct for fairness that extends even to his predecessor, which is remarkable, given that in 1995 Iacocca tried to take over Chrysler in partnership with Las Vegas billionaire Kirk Kerkorian.

"For all of the bad acquisitions that Lee made, he did buy American Motors from Renault," says Eaton. "That gave us Jeep, which is one of the strongest, most admired brands in the world, just [as it] was about to bring out the new Grand Cherokee, which was a design that completely changed the character of the sport utility market."

In dramatic contrast to "Lee," however, Eaton listened to everyone. He listened to committees of executives telling him what Chrysler was capable of doing, if only the money was available. He listened to suppliers, who told him how Chrysler could save billions of dollars by allowing them a greater hand in the engineering process at an earlier stage. He listened to the workers and met regularly with union delegates, shop stewards and ordinary assembly workers, looking for ideas to put the company back on track.

At a Jeep plant in Toledo, long infamous for production problems and a truculent union, there is nothing but praise for the changes made by Eaton. Says Bruce Baumhower, the head of the United Auto Workers local in Toledo, "I have the highest respect for Mr. Eaton. He worked hard to make the workers here part of Chrysler's team, explaining the changes they were making to improve production, asking for our ideas and asking us what needed to be done to improve conditions at the plant. Before that, we had been treated like the enemy. This used to be one of the least productive plants in the U.S. Now our productivity is nearly the highest."

Perhaps even more important, Eaton and Lutz got people at Chrysler to talk to each other. Initially, they did this by setting the example they wanted others to follow. From the first, Lutz and Eaton spent a lot of time together, often just batting around ideas. Their offices were, and are to this day, across the hall from each other, and the doors are always open. In fact, it's just as likely that you'll find Lutz in Eaton's office (or vice versa) as in his own. "There's a real informality in our relationship," says Lutz. "I'm not afraid to tell him what I think, and he's not afraid to listen. Bob has his own ideas and sometimes they are off-the-wall. But sometimes so are mine."

Both men are great believers in Tom Peters's idea of "management by walking around," and much of their time is spent roaming the Chrysler Tech Center, especially the design studios and engineering labs, which is directly connected to the executive offices. "We almost never interfere with a platform team [Chrysler's unique product development teams] decision," says Eaton, but the walkabouts serve an important dual purpose: They keep both men informed and invigorated, and it communicates their excitement and engagement to their employees.

Finally, Eaton and Lutz meet constantly, in the halls and in the lunchroom, with the rest of the executive cadre. Says

Bernard Robertson, an affable Brit who heads the truck and engineering technologies divisions, "Eaton encouraged us early on to meet on a regular basis as a group. The idea was to try to capture as much intelligence or insight as we could, from all over the place. There are so many dynamics in the business, and we all assimilate them on a daily basis from the stuff we read and hear. We place a very high premium on constant dialogue. You hear a lot of puffery about teams, but we're all together almost every day, except when we're out of town, and we talk to each other constantly."

This free-form conversation had the additional effect, Robertson says, of showing everybody that "you can't digitize this business. There is no linear programming model." This realization, in a sense, vaccinated the company against the besetting Detroit habit of building bureaucracies to systematize everything.

Another result of all the listening and talking was a thorough reassessment of a 1987 study, the work of some of the young Chrysler staffers who had joined to create what they called the Youth Advisory Committee. This group, which never numbered more than a dozen people (and sounds for all the world like a Maoist cell), persuaded Chrysler's senior management to allow it to study Honda, which was then growing rapidly and threatening to pass Chrysler as the number three U.S. automaker.

The Honda Study Team determined that Honda was everything that Chrysler was not—an open, collaborative company that encouraged debate and cooperation among its managers. The trust and the collective pool of knowledge created by this culture made Honda a more nimble carmaker, able to bring new models to market more quickly, at higher quality and lower price than Chrysler.

In a conclusion that was a stinging indictment of Iacocca's management style, the group stated that Chrysler was a company without a philsophical center, with a commitment to short-term profits at the expense of quality. In presenting the findings of the team, Reiko McKendry, a diminutive Japanese-American woman, said, "We believe that a bulldozer should be brought up to the fifth floor of the Keller building [the executive domain at Chrysler's old headquarters building] and physically knock down the walls."

The study didn't just criticize. It presented an eight-step action plan based on its findings, which was submitted to Chrysler's management in February 1988. The central recommendation was the creation of cross-functional teams that would combine engineering, design, production, sales and marketing people to produce cars, and directly involve even the most senior executives to make sure that they understood what was happening at their own company.

Iacocca endorsed elements of the plan, but not its fundamental critique. "He talked about splitting Chrysler into four individual companies," says Chris Theodore, who at the time was head of engine engineering at Jeep. "He wouldn't accept the idea of breaking down the old system." As a result, the platform team idea at the heart of the action plan had made little progress by the time Eaton came on board, says Arthur C. "Bud" Liebler, now Chrysler's vice president of marketing and the man who chaired the Honda Study Team's presentation.

Liebler, who had been assigned the delicate job of getting management to focus on and act upon the action plan, says, "There was still a lot to be done. The platform teams were an idea we were just beginning to get comfortable with when Bob [Eaton] came on board. He endorsed them strongly, and helped to make them the bedrock of the company's culture. At this point, there's no way we'd be able to even think of managing without them. Nor would we want to."

How does a platform team work and how is it different from the way Detroit normally designs and builds cars? "It's easier to answer the latter question first," says Lutz, whose office is adorned with a full-size replica of a V-12 Lamborghini engine mounted on a pedestal. "The traditional Detroit model uses product planning groups, which are staffs of several hundred people, all churning out ideas or potential ideas for new products. Once they've done that, they come up with investment estimates on the cost of making the product, and piece cost estimates and volume estimates. Now, they do this more or less on their own, without a great deal of interaction with the rest of a car company's management. And then, when they're done, the product planning staff puts a gun to the head of management, and says, 'The new product X plan will cost you $2.7 billion, will involve three assembly plants, and it's going to sell 400,000 units a year, and you will be happy with it because it will make you a lot of money. Now, if you don't like that plan, if you say $2.7 billion is too much, we can give you the $1.5 billion version, but you're not going to like it.'"

According to Lutz, there are several things wrong with

that system. First, senior management is never involved in the decision except by saying "No" at the end of the process. And the penalty for turning down a project is that a lot of time and effort will have been wasted and that the product planners will have to start all over again. That, according to Lutz, is why Ford and GM take so long to bring new cars to market, and why they are so slow to change models.

Second, says Lutz, planners have little accountability for the designs they foist on top management, once a decision is made to put a new vehicle into production. "It tended, over time, to result in programs that never made their sales volumes. You see, if the car didn't make its volume numbers, responsibility went to sales and manufacturing. The product planners could always say later on, 'Gee, we had a sensational program. It just wasn't executed well, and it was supposed to sell 400,000. Never did. Never sold more than 180,000.' "

Third, Lutz continues, there is a natural tendency among product planners to inflate sales projections. "The additional volume justifies the higher investment, and you can often work yourself out of a financial problem by just making larger assumptions on volume." For example, a part that is too costly at low volume becomes affordable as economies of scale kick in at higher sales levels. So, if a product planner wants gadgets on a new model, he predicts higher annual sales for the program.

The result, says Lutz, "is a system that is corrupt, and which has produced many spectacular failures for Chrysler, for Ford, for General Motors."

The platform system eliminates the product planning staff entirely. In its place are a small group of top executives in constant dialogue with each other, who make decisions in large part based on their feel for the market. "In order to have the level of interaction we do," says Bernard Robertson, "you have to be very open to criticism." Says Lutz, "Bob Eaton doesn't shoot the messenger when he hears something he doesn't like or understand. He knows that not every idea is right. But Bob is off-the-wall himself, sometimes. He'll say something, and we'll tell him that it's a crazy idea, and he'll pay attention to what we say. He may not change his mind in the end, but he'll spend the time explaining to you what is behind his thought processes. Do you know what kind of confidence that inspires?"

That sort of openness to risk and new ideas has helped to make Chrysler "overwhelmingly the most innovative auto company in the world," according to the management consultant Michael Hammer. They regularly meet with the executive cadre over lunch, so that ideas are kept constantly flowing, and unlike the tightly planned outputs of its competitors, the Chrysler process depends a lot on serendipity.

For example, Lutz recalls that in the mid-nineties, the four-door sports utility vehicle market was booming and the Japanese were about to begin importing compact SUVs. "Well, we're not going to do a tiny little shitty Jeep and put the Jeep name on it," Lutz recalls thinking. "But it would be nice to have a Jeep sports utility below $20,000. Nobody in the States has a Land Rover, so the idea suddenly in my mind is doing a four-door version of the Wrangler, which I discussed with my colleagues. I said, 'Hey, what if,' and at first everyone says, you know, 'why would you want to do that?'

"I sort of dropped the idea until Tom Gale brought it back, with the suggestion that we actually build the Dakar Wrangler–based four-door SUV for the Detroit [auto] show. Then, at the Detroit show, and everywhere we've shown it, it's been an absolute smash hit and everybody wants one."

It sounds like an awfully casual way to consider making a billion-dollar bet, but Eaton insists that it is better than "analysis to paralysis," the way the car industry has historically defeated innovation. Says Lutz, "If I walked into a company like Ford or GM with an idea like a four-door SUV based on the Wrangler, people would say, 'Prove that people will buy a car like that. Where's your data?' "

Eaton, like any responsible executive, asks for proof, too. But not the same kind. "A lot of what we call quantitative data, hard numbers, is really based on qualitative approaches. We take designs and we show them to the public and then we base a lot of our decisions on their responses," says Eaton. "The problem is that the process of product research becomes a substitute for product leadership. The public reacts to what we show them, and we react to their reactions. That's no way to produce great cars."

Eaton is talking about car clinics, a market research tool that shows demographically targeted groups cars that are in advanced design and planning stages, and asks them their opinion of the styling and features. Occasionally, this technique yields gold. In 1993, for example, Pontiac discovered that its core buyers wanted a return to the "widetrack" muscle cars of the 1960s and 1970s. Pontiac pushed out the wheels of its Firebird and Trans Am, created some quirky advertising that emphasized "Wider is better," and made tons of money.

Far more often, however, clinics are inconclusive and help create the kinds of indistinct and unsuccessful cars that Oldsmobile has produced for the past decade. When asked to rate cars on a scale of one to ten, most people will rate them a six or seven, and quibble about details like a grille design or taillight placement. Those comments will be sent back to the design staff, and a new grille or taillight treatment will be designed.

This begins a slow-motion disaster, says Trevor Creed, whose studio designed the hugely successful Dodge Ram full-sized pickup. First, a six or seven, according to Creed, means, "Nobody exactly loves the car but enough people can live with it," so that many product planning staffs will recommend going into production.

Second, and worse in Creed's eyes, is that the clinic process is itself poorly managed. "They show the restyled car to a completely different set of people," says Creed, who started his career at Ford of Europe, "and so they get another, completely different set of opinions. So back you go to the drawing board once again. It's endless, and you get cars that in the end are safe and formulaic and offend nobody. But they often don't sell very well."

Lutz pushes the point further. "We felt that the product planners always covered their asses. There's a huge amount of safety to it, where nobody can later be tagged as having been the person who screwed up this product. There's a risk avoidance syndrome and you tend to get a very safe product that probably won't fail abjectly, but neither is it going to succeed, and we didn't want that. We didn't think we could afford that nowadays."

One thing Eaton and Lutz agreed upon from the beginning was that a weakened Chrysler could not afford to play it safe. "As the number three carmaker, we couldn't afford to be another me-too company, because the consumer already had too many choices," says Lutz. "We had a management that was pretty much steeped in automotive expertise. We had Eaton and myself and Tom Gale and François Castaing [an engineer whom Chrysler more or less inherited when it bought American Motors from Renault] for starters. And there were enough others at a senior management level that we decided that we were going to take the responsibility for the 'what are we going to do' part of our business. Then we were going to hand the 'how do we do it' part off to the platform teams."

In fact, says Lutz, Eaton had so much confidence in the platform team approach that "in the early days Bob kept telling me to not to talk about them so much. He thought they were such a departure from the way things were done in Detroit that if other companies caught on, it would erode a lead he thought we could build up."

His intuition was sound. According to David Cole, who heads the University of Michigan's Office for the Study of Automotive Transportation (OSAT), the team method produces, "a very efficient, tightly knit decision process, coupled with a good sense of product at the highest levels of management. Chrysler's competitors are still more cumbersome in the way they get to product decisions." Moreover, says Cole, conventional product planning is likely to get it wrong more often than Chrysler's method.

For example, Ford had a great success with its original Taurus, says Cole, by benchmarking every attribute of every competitor to produce a best-in-class car. But the planning process failed when it came time to design a replacement. Every other year, OSAT asks customers what they want in cars that may be designed as much as a decade hence. "They told us they wanted three things," says Cole. "Price, space and quality. The new Toyota Camry, which competes with Taurus, went up in space and quality and came down in price. The Taurus maintained its quality, but came down in space and went up in price. The new Taurus doesn't meet customer needs as well as its competitors, and that's why Camry and the new Accord, which do, are doing so well."

Other than the shift to platform teams, the most critical single decision made by Eaton and Lutz was to turn their intuitive understandings of the car business into what they call the "polarization model" of the marketplace. Polarization is based on simple and compelling math. Counting foreign models, there are more than 150 distinct cars and models from which the U.S. car buying public can choose at any given time. The best-sellers, cars like the Honda Accord, Ford Taurus, and the Ford and Chevrolet full-sized pickup trucks, each account for no more than four percent of the fifteen million new vehicles sold each year on the U.S. car market. That means that most cars have market shares whose sales are in the 1 percent or less range. Building a car that appeals to a large percentage of the car buyer universe is therefore virtually impossible, so why bother? If you can optimize your production system to get new models to market quickly, and if you put an emphasis on interesting design, you don't have to move the needle much on any one model in order to have a positive impact on profitability.

In effect, what Eaton and Lutz realized is that a garment district dressmaker, constantly changing styles and products in response to consumer tastes, makes a better role model for a Detroit carmaker than, say, the centralized economy of Poland, circa 1970. Design a vehicle that gets the juices flowing, and it will pull in buyers who consider themselves diehard loyalists to some other make. Conversely, if you can get models out inexpensively and quickly, you can kill an unsuccessful program and move on to the next design.

What Chrysler did, says Eaton, was "Push the product envelope and buck conventional wisdom. Thus, Viper, Prowler, Ram pickup. Love them or hate them. You can't make compromises and you can't let the public have lukewarm feelings about your product. If eighty percent of the market hates your car or truck, but twenty percent says they've just got to have one or they'll die, and your market share in that category is only five percent, then you have a success on your hands."

Chrysler helped that process along by investing heavily in a computer system known as CATIA (Computer-Aided Three Dimensional Interactive Application), a system so sophisticated it enabled Boeing to design and fly a prototype of its 777 jetliner without a mockup or a wind tunnel model.

CATIA allows many people to try out new solutions on a car without building them, to see how they fit together and interact. Chrysler not only put CATIA "seats" in its engineering center—something every major car company in the world has done by now—but it placed terminals with all of its key suppliers, to bring them more intimately into the design, engineering and production processes. This was extremely important, says Cole. "Chrysler has developed great working relationships with its suppliers, which is where much of the innovation in Detroit comes from nowadays. Because they trust the suppliers, it stimulates their creative juices, and Chrysler tends to get first crack at innovations."

By allowing all the members of a platform team, along with suppliers, to work on a car simultaneously, Chrysler was able to cut its time to design and build a car from five to seven years down to twenty-three months, in the case of the Durango. Meanwhile, says Maryann Keller, the dean of auto analysts, who follows the industry for Furman Selz in New York, Chrysler's competitors continue to "throw money at something to get it done."

Chrysler's time advantage works out to a huge cost advantage. When Ford did its Contour/Mystique midsized car as a replacement for the aging Tempo, the company spent nearly $6 billion and took five years. Over that period, Chrysler brought out multiple versions of its remodeled minivan for $2.2 billion in less than three years. The hot-selling Chrysler Sebring convertible required thirty months and less than $300 million for an entirely new design, compared with the more than $700 million that Ford spent just to put a new skin on the Mustang, which involved no chassis or engine redesign.

Ford remains the most efficient of the Big Three once a model is approved and gets to the factory floor, but Chrysler is way ahead when it comes to management and design and engineering time—the most expensive part of the carmaking process. The end result is that in 1998 Chrysler enjoyed a more than $1,000 per car cost advantage over Ford and GM, according to Harbour Associates, which measures automobile company productivity.

The first and most resounding success of the polarization model was the Dodge Ram pickup. Today it's an automotive design icon. But ten years ago Ram was a dying marque, basically unchanged since its introduction in 1972. Throughout the 1980s, its market share had steadily declined, falling at times below 6 percent of the full-sized truck market (94 percent was split between Ford and Chevrolet). Nobody knew how to revive the Ram, said Robinson, since conventional wisdom had it that the loyalties of truck owners were, "almost genetic. People either bought one Chevy after another, or they bought Ford after Ford."

Pickup trucks are the Urban Cowboy's best buddy, are relatively cheap to build and are heavily customized to reflect their owners' personalities. As a result, they generate astoundingly high profit margins. That fact was not lost on Lutz, who in 1987 began arguing with Iacocca that a new truck could create a rich revenue source for Chrysler. However, just as in 1979, when Iacocca had turned down a new truck in favor of the K-car, he again brushed the idea aside. The truck design, code-named Louisville Slugger, was put on indefinite hold.

Nonetheless, designer Trevor Creed, whose main responsibility was car interiors, inherited the Louisville Slugger designs and began to tinker with them. At first, he just made minor cosmetic changes, but over the next year enough of the design was reworked so that the truck division could take the designs out and show them to clinic audiences. "We took it out to clinics and it did quite well, actually," says Bernard Robertson. "It had the attributes that the two other leaders in the marketplace had, and so its scores were, in a traditional sense, pretty good. The problem we had with it was, we had five percent of the [pickup] market and dropping, and we looked at the results and we said, 'If the market is really as brand loyal as we believe it is, why are people going to change and buy ours?' "

The answer was, they wouldn't. So Lutz and Tom Gale, Chrysler's chief designer, decided to do something radical and attention-getting. Gale went down to the truck design studio and told Creed, "Hey, instead of doing a truck that plays it safe and looks like Ford and GM, let's do something dramatic and outstanding."

Searching for inspiration, Creed found it in a book titled, simply, *Pickup Trucks*, which contained nothing but photos and silhouette sketches of pickups from the thirties, forties and fifties. Creed immediately noticed that each old truck had a singular look, unmistakably different from the others. The sketch that appealed to him most powerfully was of a Dodge Power Wagon from the late 1940s and early 1950s. The Power Wagon had those huge, squared-off fenders that farm kids used to love to ride on, while they held on to the bug-eyed front headlamps. The engine cowling was long, like the sedans of the Thirties, and a large grille that sat behind a bumper looked almost as big as a railroad engine cowcatcher.

Creed took the picture to his staff the following Monday and showed it to them. "I said, 'Start. Forget what a truck is supposed to look like and start doing stuff.' And so, all of a sudden, sketches started coming out of the designers, with the pronounced hood and dropped fenders, to simulate the pronounced nose and separate headlamps that used to be on the old Power Wagon. We had one sketch that was so close to the final production design that you'd think it was done after the car was put into production."

Early in 1989, Creed had some scale models made, but all of this was still being done in "skunkworks" fashion. And then one day, he says, "Bob Lutz and Tom Gale were going through the studio on one of their walk-throughs, and Bob saw this scale model and he fell in love with it."

Lutz fondly recalls the moment. "You can't believe how astonishing it was to see Trevor's design," he says. "It was like what a Viper would be if it was a truck. We still didn't have any money, but we decided that a little market research couldn't hurt. We were curious if the public would react as positively to it as we did."

So, in mid-1989, Chrysler took full-sized models of the design to clinics in Dallas and Ft. Worth, Texas, major full-sized truck markets and the ones where the Louisville Slugger models had been shown years earlier. Creed recalls that the new Ram with the huge grille and bumpers "got some ten out of tens, nines and tens, and a whole bunch of fours and threes. We got comments like, 'Absolutely hate it.' 'God. It's ugly.' 'It's old-fashioned. Who'd ever want to be seen in a truck like that?' But at the other end of the spectrum, we had people who said, 'I can't wait to get one. I hope you build it. It's the best-looking truck I've ever seen, reminds me of my this, reminds me of my that.' "

Armed with those reactions, Lutz and other senior managers finally persuaded Iacocca that a new Ram might indeed grab market share away from Ford and Chevy. But as the company began to translate Creed's designs into pre-production models and to do engineering work on the Ram, Chrysler began running out of cash. Creed used the delay to send a group of designers to the construction site of Chrysler's new Technology Center going up in Auburn Hills, where they took Polaroids of the interiors of the pick-ups parked by the contractors and workers. The idea was to learn how the trucks' interiors were used and customized.

"We took all the pictures and put them up on a big bulletin board and categorized them," Creed explains. "Here's where people put their coffee cups. Always on top of the dashboard. So in our design, we put a space on the top of the dashboard for cups. Another amazing thing we found out was that many of these trucks had laptop computers in there, or electronic billing machinery that was just laying on the seat, or on the floor, and so that's how the huge arm-rest came about that we put in the Ram."

A second "Best in Class," bulletin board was added. In each of the areas that had been identified as critical to the success of a truck in the Texas clinics, things like horsepower and torque, towing capacity, hauling capacity, cab dimensions, speed, handling and NVH (noise, vibration, harshness), Creed put up the specs for Chevy and Ford and then added in a superior Ram specification. "We listed all the items, and then we put the anticipated piece cost, the manufacturing effect, the quality, appearance and customer features needed to make a better truck. And what we got was a better truck in every area that customers told us was important."

Chrysler took the finished vehicle to another clinic, this time for pricing, and the ratings began to move much higher. Says Creed, "People began to feel that it had a lot of intrinsic value—in the sheet metal, in the way the hood is formed, in the fenders, in the fact that the grille went up with the hood. There's none of that on the F-150 or the Chevrolet."

Chrysler also discovered that the adamantine allegiance of truck owners to their maker was a myth. Among the 95 percent who bought one marque or the other, almost half turned out to be what were called "straddlers," people who bought a Chevy for a number of years, then switched to Ford, or vice versa. This group was made up mostly of contractors and businessmen who owned three or four trucks, and Dodge decided to concentrate its marketing on them.

With all the evidence in front of him Iacocca gave his blessing to the Ram in early July 1990, and the project was turned over to a platform team. By then, Chrysler had begun to become comfortable with the whole platform concept. Ironically, though they were passionately embraced by reformers at Chrysler, platform teams actually started out as a necessity at American Motors, where there were so few resources and so few people that Castaing and his colleagues had little choice but to work together, outside of traditional "chimneys" or "silos," as the various functional departments have come to be known by management consultants.

Almost exactly three years later, on July 19, 1993, the first Ram rolled off the assembly line, and it has been everything that Chrysler's management wanted, and more. Dodge's share of the full-sized pickup market soared to more than 20 percent in just three years. Most important, more than 85 percent of the Ram trucks Dodge sells are top-of-the line models, equipped with V-8 and V-10 engines, with expensive add-on options. As a result, Ram contributes billions to Chrysler's cash flow and bottom line. In fact, while Chrysler's overall profit is about $1,700 per car, and around $8,000 per minivan, it earns as much as $10,000 per Ram. That figure could rise even higher following Dodge's introduction of a four-door model of the Ram, the Quad Cab, in late 1997.

Perhaps more than any other Chrysler model, the Ram changed the way the company thought of itself, and the way outsiders began to perceive Chrysler. Executives and platform team members alike began to feel that, at last, Chrysler had a management that was open to their ideas, even if the ideas took awhile to work out. "The notion that we can do truly creative designs and have them looked at by senior management, not as design or car show exercises, but as the basis of cars which actually have a good chance of going into production, is what every designer dreams of," says Creed. "It's a system that recognizes talent early and rewards it, and that creates a sense of enthusiasm for your work, and a sense of mission."

The Ram, says Lutz, also provided a graphic proof that

"Leadership in this business does not always mean listening to the consumer. The consumer doesn't always know what he wants. It is a company's responsibility to present possibilities, to anticipate what the customer might like if it were offered."

Wall Street, which is the final arbiter of such things, agrees. Chrysler stock, which was selling below $10 a share in the darkest days of 1990, was selling for the equivalent of more than $80 a share ($46 a share on a 2-for-1 split-adjusted basis) in early 1998. The company has earned more money, nearly $15 billion between 1992 and 1997, than at any time in its history. With that money, Eaton has fully funded the company's pension fund, paid off billions in debt, funded several new car programs out of cash flow, and piled up a war chest of more than $7 billion. Over the same period he has raised the dividend from $.30 a share to $1.70 a share. Chrysler continues to have maintenance and reliability problems in relation to its competitors, says *Consumer Reports,* but the company is selling 50 percent more vehicles now than it did when Eaton became chairman, and more cars than in any period in its entire seventy-three-year history. "I do not intend to be like every CEO of Chrysler's past," Eaton has told anyone who will listen. "This company has gone through its last boom-and-bust cycle."

Eaton has every reason to be satisfied, even smug about Chrysler's progress under his tenure. Everything is going right. Even Reiko McKendry has gotten her wish. The fifth floor of the Keller building, Chrysler's ancien régime Highland Park headquarters building, is gone. Mahogany Row, as it was called, was a dark, dead silent, deserted corridor punctuated by closed doors. One walked soundlessly on deep carpet.

By contrast, the top floor of Chrysler's new headquarters in Auburn Hills, several miles to the north of Highland Park, is like the apex of a cathedral, with a huge glass pentastar—Chrysler's logo—catching the afternoon sunlight. There is just a thin strip of carpet down the middle of the granite floor, and everybody leaves their doors open.

Nevertheless, Eaton is anything but smug. He may run a hugely successful $61 billion corporation, but an early Friday afternoon in April 1998 finds him tieless, exhausted, sprawled sideways on a chair in his office, a tassled black loafer dangling from one foot. Eaton has just met for six hours with his thirty-five top executives. The meeting, one of several that had begun the previous Sunday, is part of an exhaustive review of the company's last five years. These are merely a prelude to an even longer set of meetings to be held at a Michigan resort, which will set Chrysler's goals and direction into the next millennium.

Endeavoring to explain how anyone could meet productively about anything for six hours, Eaton jumps out of his chair and heads for the elevator, where he descends with his visitor into the bowels of the executive tower. We exit into what looks like a high school cafeteria—cinder block walls, fluorescent lights, linoleum floors—rows of tables are surrounded by bulletin boards, on which are tacked hundreds of 3 × 5″ cards.

"This is what it's about," says Eaton, making a sweeping gesture at the unremarkable scene. These simple file cards, not some elaborate artificial intelligence program, will guide Chrysler for the next half decade. More than that, the cards are the product of the direct involvement of the thirty-five or so Young Turk executives he and Lutz have promoted into leadership, many over the heads of more senior managers, several of them out of the original Youth Advisory Committee.

This group not only has particular staff functions within the executive committee—Tom Gale heads design, Dennis Pawley heads manufacturing, for example—but these key executives also collaborate constantly, often on an ad hoc basis, to run the platform teams that design and produce Chrysler cars.

The cards are a perfect example of Eaton's collegial, unpretentious management style. They are the product of the morning's session, when all of Chrysler's executives sat and argued over their content and position. Each one lists a single factor in Chrysler's performance over the past five years. Manufacturing, purchasing, personnel, the decision to expand old plants or build new ones, billionaire Kirk Kerkorian's hostile bid for the company in 1994—every conceivable variable in Chrysler's success is here.

The idea, Eaton explains, is to account for everything that led to Chrysler's rise, rank its relative importance and systematically work to enhance those factors that helped the company, repair those that hobbled it and eliminate or minimize those beyond company control. And all of the decisions that will come out of the meetings will come from his group of managers. "I don't make decisions," he says, now that we are back upstairs, in his office. "I don't hesitate one second when I have to [make one], but my objective is not to make it."

Suddenly, the day's fatigue disappears from Eaton's

voice and his eyes. "There's only so many hours in the day," he says, "and I learned a long time ago that a single individual can't really do a hell of a lot, [except] make himself sound and look important. My philosophy is, I want to know where we're going and how we're gonna get there, and then I want to get out of the way.

"I'm not out there searching in a fog, trying to find the answer by myself," he says. "There are very few areas where I'm the most knowledgeable person in the company, and that's not the way I think the place ought to work.

"Instead, we've gone through a five-year process, still ongoing, to build a culture based on teamwork and continuous improvement, on everybody buying into what kind of company we want to be. If you have everybody spending enough time so that we know how we all think and act, I won't have to make any decisions."

Eaton knows, of course, that everybody preaches consensus and empowerment these days. But in this, as in most things, Eaton means what he says. "We've come very far in the past five years. But it won't mean a thing if we can't build a self-sustaining management group that has total and complete agreement on where they're going and why and how, that knows how to confront reality and deal with it. We weren't good at it initially. We're pretty damn good at it now. I have a saying that the person who has the most problems is going to win. That sounds like a stupid statement. What I'm really saying is the person who has identified the most opportunities for improvement, assuming he executes, is going to win."

Explains Eaton, "About four years ago, we divided the company up into three processes. They are product creation, volume production and customer acceptance. That's really all we do in this company. And those are interlocking processes. It isn't purchasing or manufacturing. If you want to improve what you're doing, you have to focus on the process and wonder if what you're doing now is the best way to accomplish that objective. Focusing on those few processes also helps break down the traditional boundaries and emphasizes teamwork.

"We want all of our executives to get experience in the process of starting a new vehicle, so we'll assign Bud Liebler [then the head of public relations], as well as the general counsel, as well as the guy who works in human relations, to get deeply involved in the start-up of a vehicle, such as the new Durango. The objective is, number one, to make sure that all of the people out there who are working recognize that we put enough importance on this that we put Bud out in the plant working on it. But it also makes Bud truly understand and solve problems at the factory level, instead of just observing. There's nothing soft and feely about this," Eaton insists. "When we're done with our discussions, these guys know where we want to go and how we want to get there, and they go back and put the action plans together to do that. This goes for every single thing we do. So I don't have to do much second-guessing, because by the time it gets to me, it's been through a very complete and thorough examination by the best minds in this company."

It's all vindication for Eaton. "If anyone had said that Chrysler would be this kind of open, dynamic place ten years ago, nobody would have believed them," he says. "But we're a totally different company from when I came, as anyone who knows Chrysler can attest. We do things differently, and our confidence is back."

Eaton has put Chrysler, a company that almost everyone had given up for dead, back on a clear path to the future. "I really do believe we've come further than any of us thought we could have come as an individual company, and I think this new merger has created a whole new horizon to strive for. We have worked as a uniform team to come where we were before this and I think we're equally as unified to go that next step." The automobile industry is going to change at least as much in the next five years as it has in the past ten. Major markets such as North America, Asia and Europe are loaded with overcapacity, and whoever fails to come up with the right answers will pay a huge price.

With the merger, Eaton is betting he has those answers. But, given his collaborative ethos, no one in the car business is more aware than he that strategic vision is nothing without the people to carry it out.

"I believe that industry in general is overmanaged and underled," Eaton declares. "Leaders are change agents, people who know where they want to go and how they want to get there. Clearly at a company there has to be a shared vision, but we try to teach people to be a leader in their own area, to know where the company wants to go, to know how that affects their area, to benchmark the best in the world and then set goals and programs to go after it. We also encourage people not only to go after the business plan objectives, but to have stretch goals. And a stretch goal by definition is a fifty-percent increase. We can improve productivity by three percent or four percent or nine percent, and do it by just getting better at what we're doing. If we go after fifty percent, something very dramatic has to happen. You have to go outside of the box."

Eaton notes that starting in 1997, the company held twenty-five symposiums for its management, of which he attended at least twenty-three. Even as the merger moves forward, changes are being instituted to strengthen Chrysler's senior management for the future. Tom Stahlkamp, for example, says, "We really are looking at changing the way we process vehicles from beginning to end here—not just in manufacturing but in the whole development of them and the selling and marketing of them." Meanwhile, design chief Tom C. Gale, now fifty-four and an executive vice president, will oversee Chrysler's product development, both the types of cars the company will build and their actual design. His job will be to find the next Vipers and minivans and slick Ram pickups.

Characteristically, in assessing the significance of this activity, Eaton diminishes his own importance. Ultimately, he says, his job is simply to vanish. "We're working very hard to build stronger leadership in this company and we'll work to do that in the new company. And so when I walk away—and I think it's the test of whether you've got a really strong team—nobody will notice that I'm gone."

Frankly, and maybe for the first time since he took charge of Chrysler, I think Bob is kidding himself.

5/Oz Nelson
The Revolutionary from Kokomo

We've all grown up with UPS. Their ubiquitous brown trucks and brown-clad drivers are as much a part of the neighborhood as the postman. In fact, many people think UPS *is* the Post Office.

I know my UPS man (who doesn't?). He's always in the neighborhood, he's always working, and when someone sends me a package he's the one who brings it over. Once, passing him on my way to work, I stopped by his truck and asked him what he thought of Oz Nelson. He put down the package he had in his hand. "Let me tell you something about Oz Nelson," he said. "He had a vision of the future and he told us drivers, get out there and to hell with the rules—do what you need to do to make the customer happy. If you go to pick up a package and it won't be ready for twenty minutes, fine, come back in twenty minutes.

"You tell Oz Nelson that I'm not only a driver, I'm a union shop steward, too. And I think he saved this company. This company made more than a billion dollars in 1997, and that's thanks to Oz Nelson."

Big. Bald. Bespectacled. Given to brown suits and exclamations like "Gee whiz" and "Aw, shucks." Kent "Oz" Nelson looks more like a Rotarian middle-manager from Kokomo, Indiana (his hometown), than a high-tech turnaround artist. Even his nickname, derived from Ozzie Nelson, the bland dad of fifties television, calls forth images of small-town contentment and obscurity. But from 1989 to 1996, Oz Nelson was CEO of the United Parcel Service, the world's largest package delivery company. And he quietly turned UPS on its head.

Nelson took UPS, a $22 billion-plus company, whose 330,000 employees move more than twelve million parcels a day, from the horse-and-buggy era into the cyberworld, transforming it into one of the most technologically advanced companies on the planet.

Jeffrey A. Sonnenfeld, a former professor at Emory University, in Atlanta, Georgia, and the foremost student of the company, says, "Oz is amazing. He's a nineteenth-century guy with a twenty-first–century mind. UPS was in a position where it could have been destroyed—it was time—but instead it changed, it renewed itself, and that in some ways is harder than just turning a company around."

It's a view echoed by Wall Street. "Nelson played an integral role in the decision-making process in bringing the company into the twentieth century," says Paul R. Schlesinger, analyst at Donaldson Lufkin & Jenrette. "The downsizing and streamlining that they have done at the management level, without missing too many beats financially and competitively, it's just astounding."

Oz's excellent adventure began in the early 1980s. UPS, a famously insular place, scanned the horizon and saw that times had changed—and were changing even faster. Competition had arrived in the form of Federal Express of Memphis and Roadway Package System of Pittsburgh. They had better technology and a lower cost structure, and they simply went out and began winning business from UPS's largest and most profitable accounts—companies like General Motors and Kodak.

For the first time in its history UPS, which has always looked as quaint as a Norman Rockwell painting, began to be perceived that way.

"We had to change," Oz remembers. "We always thought we knew what was best for customers, and when they came to us and asked for something special that's what we told them. 'We know what's best, and one price fits all.' Well, we were wrong. Unfortunately, we weren't a company that was accustomed to doing anything other than our way."

That way of doing business had a long and honorable heritage. Back in 1907, James E. "Jim" Casey, an enterprising nineteen-year-old in Seattle, Washington, saw a business in the fact that few private homes had telephones. So personal messages had to be carried by hand and packages had to be delivered the same way. (The U.S. Postal Service began the parcel post system only in 1913.) Casey sat down in a basement office with his brother George and a few other teenagers, and they founded the American Messenger Company—a bicycle messenger and delivery service. They began with just two bicycles and $100, but Casey offered customers courtesy, reliability, round-the-clock service and low rates. The business prospered.

In 1913, Casey merged his operation with one run by Evert "Mac" McCabe, to form Merchants Parcel Delivery, which soon had three of Seattle's largest department stores as regular customers. The last of the founders, Charlie Soderstrom, soon joined the firm to manage the growing fleet of delivery vehicles, which now included automobiles.

From the 1920s up until the outbreak of World War II, Merchants Parcel Delivery expanded to all the major West Coast cities and began a consolidated delivery service in the New York City area. (Consolidated delivery, using one vehicle to deliver all packages destined for a given neighborhood, was itself a Merchants Delivery invention.) In 1925, the company changed its name to United Parcel Service: "United" because shipments were consolidated, and "Service" because, as Soderstrom observes, "Service is all we have to offer."

The stock market crash of 1929 and the ensuing Great Depression forced the company to fold its fledgling air service. But it also enabled the founders to buy back all its outstanding stock, worth more than $2 million, which it had issued to a New York investment bank earlier in the decade. From then on, Casey was determined to keep UPS a private company, immune to outside influence and the vicissitudes of the stock exchanges. UPS would become one of the nation's most secretive privately held companies, until Oz took over and instituted a kind of corporate glasnost. "This was a company that for a long time never talked to the press," Sonnenfeld says. "People used to joke that it was some sort of cult."

After the war, as the country took to the suburbs and the automobile, shoppers quickly became accustomed to taking their purchases home with them. In response, UPS began to extend its reach, fighting a state-by-state battle against restrictions that had prevented it from operating in many parts of the country. In fact, it took UPS until 1975 to win the right to operate in all forty-eight contiguous states. It was during this period of steady expansion that Oz Nelson signed up.

In 1959, Oz Nelson graduated from Ball State University in Muncie, Indiana. His fraternity brothers told him about UPS. There was, he recalls, "a chance to get a good job, and I jumped at it." Two days after graduation, he began working for the only employer he would ever have.

Oz's father had been raised on a farm and his formal education ended in the fourth grade, when the Great Depression forced him to find a job to help support the family. He spent most of his life as an industrial worker, eventually becoming a superintendent at a plant that made aluminum frames for plate glass storefronts. Oz's mother had two years of high school and never worked outside the home.

For Oz, as for many generations of men and women

from modest backgrounds, UPS became a sort of university, a place where their talents and commitment could be recognized and rewarded over the long haul. Up until the 1960s, UPS executives invariably started as drivers. It was an article of faith, as he says, that "Driving is hard work, you got to produce every day. I can't think of a better way to learn what an organization is about." He began in sales and slowly worked his way through the organization. In fact, Nelson, who, with his Midwestern vowels and chipped-tooth smile could easily be mistaken for a UPS driver, was the first CEO who had never driven for the company, a matter of considerable internal controversy at the time of his promotion.

David Kanouse, sixty-five, knew Oz when he used to drop by the UPS facility in Kokomo in the early sixties. "We drivers were paid three bucks for every new account we could find, and Oz was one of the sales guys who roamed around and would come over and collect the leads," says Kanouse, who retired as a driver three years ago and still lives in Kokomo.

"He was this tall and skinny guy, who joked a lot and got along well with people," Kanouse recalls. He adds that when Nelson was named CEO a quarter century later, "I didn't believe it when I heard it—no one who knew him then could believe it."

Kanouse gives Oz high marks during his tenure at the top, though. "Guys liked him, and I never heard a derogatory remark about him. And from what I hear, I don't think there would have been a strike last year, if Oz had still been the CEO," he says. "Oz as the CEO had a little better way of working with the people; he respected them a little more, I think."

Over the next two decades, Nelson rose to become the company's top marketing officer, and in 1982 he was asked by then-Chairman George Lamb and CEO Jack Rogers (who would succeed Lamb in 1984), to become the chief financial officer of UPS. Nelson swears his first thought was, " 'Gee, they must think I'm more capable than I think I am, because I don't think I can do that job.' And I said I'd try it."

He was promoted in 1986 to senior vice president and then to vice chairman in 1989. Just before year's end, Oz Nelson was named chairman and CEO of the company where he had spent his adult life. "It's funny working for Jack Rogers, who I truly love and admire," Nelson says. "He's just a great guy, but he isn't very verbal. Jack came to me one day and he said, 'You know, Oz, I've decided to re- tire in a few months. I think they, the board, probably want you as vice chairman at the next board meeting.' And that was the first time anybody had said anything to me.

"I just sat there and said: 'I guess—if that's what they want.' I didn't know how to react to it. Nobody ever said another word to me. And they elected me vice chairman at the next board meeting, and still nobody told me I was going to be CEO. It just sort of happened."

In 1990, as Oz settled in, UPS's perennially sunny skies darkened. The company's profit margins were sliding toward 4 percent from nearly 7 percent in 1988, testimony to the impact FedEx and RPS were having.

People *trying* to compete with UPS was nothing new, Oz notes. "Every five or six years somebody tried to mount an attack on us. After two or three or four years, they'd fall by the wayside. They just weren't able to compete. And then around 1985, all of a sudden along came a company called RPS, and clearly they did their homework. They had done a very intelligent analysis of our strengths and weaknesses, and were, in a very intelligent way, knocking off our most profitable customers in regional areas whose packages not only generated the most revenue, but the most profitable revenue.

"And after a short period of time, maybe too long, it became apparent to me that they were going be successful. They were very selective about who they offered service to, and they only took shippers who had certain kinds of deliveries to the best delivery stops, whose packages were heavy and averaged high revenue because of it. And they didn't take any local packages, even within 150 miles at that time. No intrastate, so it wasn't any of the urgent stuff. And they took that segment of the business and priced it by discounting off of our rate charts. Then, instead of hiring employees, they decided to have independent contractors, and required them to buy their own trucks, and then paid them less wages than we did, and no benefits on top of it. They were walking into our best customers and cutting our prices twenty-five to thirty percent."

Nelson responded by ordering a sweeping examination of UPS's business methods and appointed four senior executives—sales and marketing chief John W. Alden, international head Donald W. Layden, engineering guru Charles L. Schaffer, and chief financial officer Edwin A. Jacoby—to determine how the company should answer its rivals.

"You know, I had read about other companies going through change, and I thought they must have been really fouled up," Nelson says. "And here we were doing a good deal of these things ourselves."

UPS's unique culture—sometimes described as half-socialism, half-Quaker meeting—had given the company great stability (a majority of the company's full-time employees will spend their entire careers there), but also created an enormous amount of inertia and complacency. "Our success came from replicating the same thing over and over again," Oz says. "We had this image of ourselves that we were the best in the world because we knew we were, and we were hard-pressed to find people who could make us better. We would bring in consultants, and they would look at us, and they would make suggestions that did not seem to make sense to us, and we wouldn't do them.

"So, we got to the point where we didn't listen as well as we should have. And people started coming after us and competing with us and taking pieces of our business. If you don't react as a leader in crisis, you endanger the life of the company. And what we faced was a crisis. It was a shock to our operations people that we couldn't solve this problem of competition by simply working harder, being more efficient. But being more efficient wasn't the answer to that problem. It's providing the services the customers needed. We weren't used to thinking that way and had to change it."

The problem was that UPS was the "operating" company par excellence, one where, Oz says, employees "felt largely that [UPS's] success or failure would rest on its ability to provide high levels of reliable service and high levels of productivity at good rates." Suddenly, these old-fashioned virtues would not be sufficient. Oz's insight was that the very competition that was imperiling his company's business future was also the Archimedean lever he could use to move his huge and conservative organization. Pointing out that FedEx and RPS were "eroding some of our business and attracting some of our large customers," Oz observes, he could then "enunciate to our supervisors and managers that we now had to add . . . the ability to apply technology, more flexible servicing for customers, listen harder to customers and give them more of what they wanted, instead of what we deduced was best for them and us. It was an educational process that was installed by lots of discussions with management at all levels . . . and real-life examples were popping up from our competition for our people to see, new products that we weren't in a position to offer. It became pretty obvious to all that we had to change and the team became receptive, became ready to embrace change."

Oz's first strategic step was to reach out to customers. For years, the marketing team had consisted of just seven people. By 1992, the staff had increased to 175 and was handling 6,000 corporate inquiries a year. Next came face-to-face interviews with 25,000 customers to find out what services and products they needed.

After the interviews, UPS decided it had better start doing business differently. For instance, the company altered its seemingly ancient loop procedure, which informed shippers when a package would be picked up. If it wasn't ready—sorry, try again tomorrow. Today, when a customer wants, say, a later pickup, he gets it. The company began offering three-day guaranteed delivery at 20 percent less than second-day service.

Nelson recalls, "Our marketing people went out and talked to the customers, along with our customer service people, and really listened. And said, well, maybe this isn't the way I want to run the operation, but if it's what the customer needs and wants, I'd better do it."

Terrence M. Golomb, Kodak's manager of worldwide transportation services, remembers that back in 1991 he was thinking of dumping UPS. "Every time we would ask them about special services or discounts, I would hear back the same thing: 'It's not in our best interest,' " Golomb says. "Well, that's not what I was hearing from their competitors."

UPS under Nelson responded to Golomb's complaints and placed a full-time service representative at Kodak's Rochester headquarters. They also began showing the company how to cut its shipping bills and offering discounts.

"The company's operations always have been top-notch, but for much of its history, it insisted that customers fit the system, rather than using its system to respond to customer requirements," says Peter Bradley, the editor in chief of *Logistics Management and Distribution Report,* an industry newsletter. "That changed to a marked degree during Nelson's watch. Once UPS recognized the competitive threats, it responded aggressively and became the stronger for it. And its execution was superb."

Surprisingly, the headquarters-driven overhaul of the corporate culture met little resistance from managers and supervisors in the field. Retraining helped. More than five hundred managers were sent to Michigan State University's business school in East Lansing for week-long seminars, in which professors coached them to think in terms of customer service.

"I wasn't sure it was going to be as easy as it was," says Nelson. "When several of us became convinced that we were going have to deal differently with customers—perhaps give them more respect than we had—and make decisions differently, and do a better job of listening, frankly, I wasn't sure how effective we were going to be."

What Oz discovered, though, was that the employees were ready for the change, in part because all UPS managers and supervisors own shares in the company; indeed many have their life's savings tied up in it, thanks to the company's profit-sharing plans. Every year, 15 percent of UPS's pretax profit is used to buy company stock that is distributed to employees, from entry level supervisors on up. Nonmanagement employees, including drivers and pilots, may purchase UPS stock, and more than 100,000 have done so. There's no public market for UPS shares, but based on what it pays to buy back shares from those retiring or quitting, the value of stock has risen at a compound annual rate of more than 23 percent in the past decade.

"We have 25,000 owner-managers who have virtually every cent they own invested in stock of this company," says Nelson, who owns several million dollars' worth of UPS stock. "They knew that if we didn't change, somebody would, and there'd go your life savings.

"We were being outdone in some areas, and people weren't used to that. As always, change meant that lots of people would have to tackle their jobs differently. We had to change the mindset of our people, which we did. In fact, watching our people embrace the change has been the most rewarding thing I've experienced."

Linda Kaboolian, a professor at the Harvard Business School, recalls that a few years ago she showed a group of executives a short film about UPS—the boxy brown trucks, orderly warehouses, and the disciplined, uniformed, work-force in regulation socks and undershirts. When asked, none of the executives said they would like to be the CEO of UPS. "They saw UPS as staid and plodding," Kaboolian says.

It was a reasonable assumption. This, after all, is a quirky company; it washes its 75,000 brown trucks and its fleet of jets regularly to maintain an image of cleanliness and orderliness. It also has a strict code about its uniforms and personal appearances. "A uniform isn't a mask like some people think," Nelson says. "It's a badge of dedication." The past, in particular, has always been revered at UPS; Pullman brown has remained the corporate color even though Pullman cars have long since disappeared. And founder Jim Casey has been turned into an icon. Indeed, a bronze plaque hangs above the spot in Seattle where he founded UPS.

Given this sort of cultural heritage, it makes sense that when UPS, historically phobic about technology, decided to take the plunge, they found a way to get the founder's blessing. In 1987, at the company's eightieth manager's meeting, the 25,000 on hand were treated to an amazing sight: a Zelig-like video of the long-dead Casey having a conversation with then-CEO Jack Rogers about the need for modernization. It was a prototypical UPS moment: the past, in the form of the founder's electronic ghost, was raised to ease fears about the future.

Says Nelson, "We had to take a good, hard look at our use of technology and how we could use it to increase service offerings to our customers, differentiate more from the Post Office and also match service features of people like Federal Express and RPS.

"This was very hard on our operations people, in particular," he says, given the company's tradition of penny-pinching that ran all the way back to 1907. "The mindset [was] to compete with the rates of the Post Office, which were money-losing rates and always have been, forgetting First Class mail, which subsidizes the whole package business. We were driven to control costs.

"In fairness, in the past we had done the human engineering thing fairly well. I mean, nobody can use people better than we could. And every time we put in automated systems, it cost a lot of money and slowed us down."

The remarkable thing about Oz, according to Professor Sonnenfeld, was that he saw that, despite the negative historical experience, technology was crucial to the company's future. And he was willing to bet big on it. Upon becoming CFO, Nelson had asked Rogers if he could ride herd on UPS's technology efforts, as well as learn his new job. Given the internal resistance to technology spending, he says, "I think he was happy to have somebody who'd want to do that."

When Oz took over the computer and technology groups, they consisted of about one hundred people. Within three years, the number had grown to about four thousand. "We went out, hired people, or trained people, promoted people, sent our own people to school to get them upgraded," Nelson says. "And we have created one of the biggest computer operations in the world."

Frank Erbrick, the company's recently retired chief information officer, pointed out the scope of the change. Technology, he says, meant that UPS would no longer just be moving packages, it would be moving huge amounts of information in real time.

"Customers can now use UPS to connect to their customers, to receive orders electronically, have UPS ship the order, tell them when it was received and that it's okay to send an invoice," Erbrick says. "That's a big change from just being the back-end guys who delivered the boxes."

Nelson went out on a limb and hired Michael Dertouzos, a professor of computer science at Massachusetts Institute of Technology, to help revamp the company's computers and technology. "He cost an unbelievable amount of money," Nelson says. "I mean it just killed me to have to pay him, he was so expensive. And he's not the biggest diplomat in the world, either, but boy is he smart."

Dertouzos, who runs MIT's Laboratory for Computer Science, has fond memories of consulting for UPS, and why not—it's not often an academic has a chance to reshape one of the largest companies in the world. "It was the most impressive company I have seen in my life," he says. "The whole ethos of UPS is unbelievable. They were hardworking, motivated, organized. Oz was on top of everything. He was very understanding, and supportive and knew what he needed. He knew it before a lot of people, too, and that was important. He was an early bird."

Among the devices Dertouzos and the technology team dreamed up was a voice box that tells package sorters where to place a package on a truck. "They load their trucks in the morning, and it takes time to read the codes and place them in the van in a way so that the driver can get them out fast when they are on their routes," Dertouzos says. "So, we created a bar code reader that speaks to the loader and tells them based on the zip code and other information. It enables a loader to do four or five hundred packages an hour. You may be spending a half billion a year on technology and information services, but you are saving a billion with devices like this."

Nelson says Dertouzos "opened my eyes so wide about what was possible. Now some of our technology guys saw it, but they thought it was going to be too expensive, or they didn't want to do it now. They wanted to slow it down, and do other things first." The argument continued until, finally, Nelson felt that he thoroughly understood all the issues. At that point, he recalls, "I understood what had to happen. I called the team in one day and said, 'This is what we're going to do. It's no longer debatable. We're going to get there as fast as we can. And you're responsible for making it happen.' "

Out of Oz's missionary efforts in this area came the DIAD, a handheld electronic clipboard/cellular telephone that's connected to the company's central computers and is used by drivers to track packages in real time. The device also digitizes the signature of the person receiving the package. "In my opinion, that was the most important thing we have done in the area of technology," Nelson says. "When they came out, no one had ever seen something like that."

Nelson was also the catalyst for the construction of the Chicago Area Consolidated Hub (CACH), a massive 1.9-million-square-foot state-of-the-art automated sorting and delivery system. "It's known as 'the house that Oz built,'" says Mike Johl, a senior manager at CACH. One of the most important technological innovations at UPS during Nelson's reign was the Maxicode, a two-dimensional symbol that looks like a fingerprint and has encoded in it about one hundred characters of information. The code, which tells UPS all kinds of things about the package's sender and receiver, contains about as much data as nineteen inches of a standard code bar and can be read even on the bent or topsy-turvy surfaces of packages on conveyor belts moving at more than five hundred packages a minute. Maxicode labels are crucial to CACH, where UPS sorts 177,000 parcels per hour.

During the Nelson years, UPS also lavished money on jets and advanced technology for its air delivery system, which is today the eighth largest "airline" in America. "It has been successful beyond our wildest dreams," Nelson says proudly. "I think we're the most efficient airline in the world, and the safest airline in the world, including any passenger airline. Nobody can touch us. The FAA tells us that, too. They inspect us and say, 'Gee, you guys ought to be in the passenger business. We don't have anybody this good.' Actually, we do have a small passenger charter business. And no, the flight attendants don't wear brown uniforms."

The impetus for expanding the air fleet was "absolutely, positively," Federal Express, which had quickly become as much of a threat in the skies as RPS had been on the ground. Federal Express started out purely as a next-day air service, a business UPS wasn't even in. But, says Oz, "We knew that they would begin looking around and eventually take on our second-day delivery service and then lastly our ground service. So, we decided we'd better go after them. We started a service, and it was successful, not from the first day forward, but after sixty days or so."

Since then, the company has expanded air delivery services throughout Europe, Latin America and Asia, and the company has, in a remarkably short time, become known as a global high-tech player. Overall, from the time Oz became CFO, until his retirement, UPS spent an estimated $2 billion on technology initiatives. In the process, Oz transformed the attitudes and habits of his huge workforce, turning UPS itself in the public imagination from a throwback to a cutting edge institution. All in all an astonishing achievement for any CEO to have overseen, much less a self-described regular guy from Kokomo.

Nelson's technology investments, Bradley says, were "breathtaking in scope and have revolutionized the way UPS does business. The DIAD, for instance, totally replaced an antiquated paper system. In addition, much of the logistics service that UPS provides its customers is driven by its technology."

Paul M. Cole, the national director for customer connections solutions with Ernst & Young, and coauthor, with

Robert E. Wayland, of *Customer Connections: New Strategies for Growth,* calls Nelson "one of those rare CEOs who truly deserves the title visionary."

"UPS's shift from a one-size-fits-all strategy to that of a firm eager to partner with its customers and develop customized solutions is one of the most remarkable and underreported transformations in U.S. history," he says.

Cole cites UPS's relationship with the Gateway 2000 computer company in creating a virtual assembly-line-in-a-truck pallet called DOCKMERGE. "Previously, all of a customer's components, such as printers, modems, monitors, et ceteras, went to Gateway's facility to be shipped to the customer even though Gateway only customizes the computer. Using information technology, UPS and Gateway collaboratively figured out a way to have all the components make the shortest possible trip but arrive together at the customer's premises. In fact, they may never be put together until the last leg in the brown truck.

"This sort of technology is supported by spending $500 million a year on information technology, about a third of which are for customer automation," he says. "Although people tend to think of FedEx as the technology leader in the sector, UPS has caught up and in several areas has taken the lead. This level of spending was begun under Nelson and Erbrick and initially was done partly on faith because IT [the information technology division] couldn't provide the detailed cost-benefit analysis demanded of all UPS projects. But Nelson sensed it was the direction of the future."

And he appears to have put UPS in an excellent position to remain one of the dominant delivery services. "It has a global network, first-rate technology, and a breadth of services, all in large part because of Nelson," Peter Bradley says. "Should electronic commerce come even close to becoming as important as we all seem to expect, UPS, along with a few other providers, is in an excellent position to take advantage of that." (Note the UPS button on Internet search engines like Yahoo as evidence of that.)

As the company's current CEO, James P. Kelly, puts it, "Oz was tremendous at leading his team. He turned the entire focus of the company around."

Looking back on his forty-year career, Nelson says he picked up most of his leadership skills on the job, and through the UPS culture of discipline and meritocracy. "I really strongly feel that leadership at UPS is provided by a lot of people, and at every level," he says. "I saw leadership in the highest degree when I worked for the district back in Indiana."

UPS is the sort of place, he says, where those who are successful are generally those who identify to a high degree with the kind of company it is and with the image it projects to the rest of the world. "Leadership has a lot to do with setting examples. Basically, it's just so many little things. It's just getting to work on time, and getting to work every day. It is about just being honest in the way you conduct yourself. I love the kind of leaders you can see right through. If they say something, you know they mean it. You don't have to worry about if there's some other agenda.

"It's also about being supportive to the people who deserve support, and rewarding people who do well, and helping those who are having a tougher time."

He speaks from experience. Many years ago, Nelson learned that one of his two young sons—today grown and a successful businessman—had cerebral palsy. "I took our son home and I talked to my wife for a while, and I went back to the office," he recalls. "And then I'm sitting in the office, and the district manager walked by my office, and he said, 'What's wrong?' And I told him. And he said, 'Close up your desk, get in your car, and go home.' He said, 'You should be with your wife,' and I should have been. And I went home." Later, a fellow employee helped the Nelsons give his son the extra care he required.

Nelson readily agrees that his selfless style is a perfect match for the low-ego corporate culture of UPS. "It would be very difficult for someone who's not a team player and a personable person to get very far in our organization, because, you know, we really are a participatory management company. There are about thirteen people on the UPS management committee, and I'd say the rookie has been there about twenty-five years. And they all started at the bottom and worked their way up. The CEO now was hired as a driver in New Jersey. Our chief counsel went to law school at nights and started as a part-time sorter for us. And we've all learned the job through a series of progressions, and I think that gives us the advantage that our competitors don't have.

"For example, if our top management were to make a decision they would understand that impact on all the jobs up through the organization, because they've done it," he says. "If you're a driver, and your supervisor has not only

done the job that you do, and done it so well he got promoted, you tend to listen to what they say. It works the
other way, too. If you've done that job, you know what it
takes to do it well, and there's a certain respect that goes
back to those people."

Some things, it seems, will never change at UPS.

6/Michael Bonsignore
Taking the Heat

In February 1995, Michael Bonsignore, CEO of Minneapolis-based Honeywell Inc., found himself on the cover of *Barron's* magazine. There he was—or rather, there was his caricature—slumped over and sweating in a sauna, wearing only a towel and a foolish grin. "Turning up the Heat" ran the headline.

It was not, to say the least, an upbeat story. One unnamed securities analyst was quoted saying, "The time for excuses at Honeywell has run out. If [Bonsignore and his team] can't do better, I guess we'll all be looking for someone else who can." That someone, the story hinted, might be a hungry competitor, perhaps General Electric or Allied

Signal. Or a "stockholder putsch" might force Bonsignore's summary dismissal.

The same week, *Business Week* weighed in with "Not So Sweet Times at Honeywell." The piece focused on Honeywell's lackluster 1994 (net revenues down 13 percent), and on its "clubby, paternalistic culture," which had survived six restructurings in eight years. "Investors are growing impatient," the magazine warned, "and the board is upping pressure to show results." A hapless shareholder sighed, "Sometimes I wonder if management knows what it's doing."

What made these articles doubly humiliating was that, just weeks before their publication, Bonsignore had unveiled an ambitious three-year revenue growth plan before a meeting of securities analysts and institutional investors. In the first year alone, he promised to boost earnings per share from $2.15 to $2.40. Unfortunately, recalls Michael R. Robinson, then Honeywell's vice president for investor relations, "By that time, we only had maybe one or two buy recommendations left," among the analysts, and the audience was not only unimpressed—it was hostile. The rosy projections were seen as little more than a public relations ploy on the part of a management team going nowhere. "They just blew us right out of the water," Bonsignore says. "We had no credibility."

Wall Street's frustration was understandable. Between 1989 and 1992, Honeywell's revenue had plateaued at roughly $6 billion, while profits contracted from $550 million to below $250 million. Over the same years, earnings per share sank from $3.60 to $1.78; return on equity from 33 to 14 percent.

All in all, Honeywell appeared to have reached the end of a glorious century-long run that began in 1885, when a Swiss immigrant invented a "damper flapper," to regulate the heat of coal furnaces. The company followed up with a seemingly endless series of temperature control devices, aggressively marketed to a broadening range of domestic and industrial customers. The infiltration of technology into every crevice of twentieth-century life only increased demand for Honeywell's expertise, which proved remarkably adaptable. By the 1950s, its products ranged from its famous round home thermostats, to products for oil-processing plants, to aircraft autopilots.

Honeywell had become an American institution, and began to behave like one. Entrepreneurial and marketing ingenuity were supplanted by lumbering bureaucracy. This helped create a major disaster in the "Go-Go" 1960s, when Honeywell entered the computer business because it seemed to promise easy and rapid growth, although it bore little or no relationship to the company's traditional business.

It took more than a decade for Honeywell to earn its first profits on mainframe computers—a market segment that soon contracted as newer technologies came to market. Despite hundreds of millions of dollars in R&D spending, Honeywell had just 2 percent of the market in general-use computers by 1984, and the computer division's annual losses routinely exceeded $10 million at a time when the industry as a whole was rolling in profits.

Meanwhile, the rest of the company plodded along, with an increasing percentage of revenues (as much as 40 percent at one point) coming from military contracts. Honeywell had begun working with the Air Force during World War II and had taken on some weapons-system and ordnance production, all of which burgeoned during the Reagan-era military buildup. It was never among the dominant defense contractors (never even among the top ten), however, and when government spending slowed and behemoths like Lockheed began to fight for an ever larger slice of a shrinking pie, Honeywell found itself unable to compete.

In 1985, Edson Spencer, Honeywell's CEO from 1974 to 1987, sold the computer business, spun off the defense contracting and began the agonizing and ugly process of slashing the workforce from 94,000 to 50,000. This last job was completed by Spencer's successor James Renier, who ran the company from '87 to '93. All of this, combined with a series of financial restructurings necessitated by the downsizing, demoralized Honeywell's remaining workers. As one veteran field manager recalls, it was a time when people stopped thinking of themselves as a part of Honeywell, and simply concentrated on not losing their jobs.

Renier also opened up the succession process, ending a longstanding tradition in which the CEO hand-picked his successor and rubber-stamped the decision.

When the succession race began, Bonsignore had two rivals. One was Larry Moore, who had come to Honeywell via its acquisition of the Sperry aerospace company ten years before. Highly respected, Moore's primary skills were technical and financial. Christopher Steffan, on the other hand, was an outsider brought in under Renier to mastermind the company's downsizing. He was Wall Street's favorite, someone regarded as willing to make tough decisions. But Steffan left for Kodak when it became clear he wouldn't get the top slot right away.

In fact, choosing between Moore and Bonsignore took the better part of a year. Each board member interviewed both candidates, and in the end they opted for Bonsignore because he had an encyclopedic knowledge of Honeywell and an intangible combination of charisma and determination. "It was his leadership skills that really impressed us," recalls William Donaldson, a longtime Honeywell board member and, as cofounder of Donaldson Lufkin & Jenrette, a Wall Street heavyweight. "He's a Navy guy through and through." His skill set may not have been as strong on number-crunching, but the board felt he knew how to communicate his goals and how to inspire rank-and-file employees to achieve them. "Openness" is the word that board member James Howard, CEO of Northern States Power Company, uses again and again in describing Bonsignore's personal style. "That's something that inspires confidence, then and now," he adds.

As Bonsignore and his colleagues past and present tell it, his character—and his leadership style—took shape in the U.S. Naval Academy, from which he graduated in 1963. Leadership training at Annapolis focused on developing competence and projecting confidence, and using those personal attributes to inspire subordinates to achieve clear objectives. There was very little managerial mystification. For Bonsignore, a rather unassuming and straightforward young man from upstate New York, it all fit like a glove. "You know that computer industry term 'WYSIWYG'—What You See Is What You Get?" says E. D. Grayson, Honeywell vice president and general counsel. "That's Mike. He doesn't have any secrets. If he has something on his mind, he tells you."

Joining Honeywell as a twenty-eight-year-old engineer in 1969, Bonsignore, who is quite literally tall, dark and handsome, proved to be a great salesman. He rose quickly into the ranks of management and in 1982 got his break, relocating to Brussels to assume the presidency of Honeywell Europe. Colleagues during that time recall how he hopscotched around the continent building confidence—and loyalty—at the various national units. Lawrence Stranghoener, today vice president and chief financial officer of Honeywell, had transferred to Germany in 1984, and was surprised to be summoned almost immediately to Brussels to meet Bonsignore in person. "He just wanted to meet me, to let me know he knew who I was and that I was well thought-of," Stranghoener recalls. "It made me feel, obviously, very, very good about things. I'll never forget it. It was like we were old friends."

When he returned to Minneapolis in 1987, Bonsignore had risen to become chief of international operations as well as the company's core home and building control business. Both areas outperformed the rest of the company.

So, a year after the search had begun, Honeywell had as its new CEO a virtual "lifer." This did not sit well with Wall Street, which wanted anything but another product of a moribund corporate culture. Still, if nothing else, Bonsignore's long service had given him a clear sense of the real state of affairs at Honeywell. "Our businesses had not grown for so long our people began to believe that they would *never* grow," he says. Honeywell was a name known and respected worldwide, yet the place was simply "lifeless," says CFO Stranghoener. "Anyone who had worked here for any length of time had some degree of skepticism, just because of the atmosphere. It was not a place that you felt real good about."

In addition, the lengthy search for a new CEO had only increased the anxiety throughout the company. "The uncertainty about the transition had really caused the company to slip into a wait-and-see mode," notes E. D. Grayson. And no wonder. "We'd gone from ninety thousand employees to fifty thousand," says Bonsignore. "They saw whole businesses sold, all these executives disappearing. People were really pretty shell-shocked."

This was the core issue Honeywell had to face; cost cuts and cultural changes would be meaningless if Bonsignore couldn't make revenue and profits grow again. Nor would productivity gains achieve more than limited results. Profitable growth could only come from innovations, new ways of selling, new technologies to sell. He likens Honeywell to a veteran athlete who still had great potential, but, "through a series of injuries and different signals from different coaches about what his training regimen ought to be, the veteran athlete had never really been able to achieve this Olympic status. All the ingredients were there."

Bonsignore decided to meet the lassitude and inertia head-on. The widespread belief that Honeywell had plateaued as a $6 billion company, he said, was "unacceptable. The top line has to change." But Honeywell was a stagnant company and it operated like one. Process and politics reigned over practice and performance. There were redundant management layers, lots of oversight and second-guessing and enough committees to ensure that decisions could always be tabled for further discussion. Gayle Pincus, a Phoenix-based manager in Honeywell's industrial business, recalls the period as one in which every unit was a fiefdom. "It was hard to relate to Honeywell as a whole," she says. "We didn't have the same stake in it." Making things worse, each fiefdom's leadership was setting its own performance goals, and had little incentive to set those goals high. This was doubly true because their compensation bonuses were often tied to hitting the goals they set for themselves.

All this had to change, swiftly and unmistakably, and Bonsignore's operational overhaul could have been taken straight out of a leadership course back at the Naval Academy. It was based on a few commonsense axioms. If you want people to work hard and show initiative:

Give your troops clear goals, and build in real accountability.

Communicate, motivate and inspire. Communicating with business units simply wasn't a priority for top management in the past. As a result, each unit tended to operate virtually as a separate company, with no real sense of belonging to a larger entity called "Honeywell," which had a broader, more inclusive view of the priorities and health of the entire corporate body.

Get out of the way. Once goals are clear, accountability is real, and everyone is motivated, the front line is the place to make decisions.

Invest in your people. Make sure they have the skills and tools to do what you ask of them.

These were simple, straightforward and reasonable ideas. Even at the time, it's unlikely that many of Honeywell's managers would have disagreed with them. The challenge was to give these management chestnuts life at a global company whose past was more real than its future.

It was not an easy moment, and Bonsignore recalls that he soon began to feel like a captain desperately turning a wheel to keep his vessel off the rocks. "And I thought, 'God, is the wheel even *connected* to anything?' "

■

Bonsignore's first step was by fiat. He began assessing his business units through something called "peer-group performance." In the past, Honeywell's innumerable departments within its three primary business units—home and building control; industrial control; and space and aviation—had used their own past performance as the only benchmark. It was all based on "making plan," he says, "and plan was put together through a bottoms-up negotiation that was excruciating. It took a tremendous amount of time. I would say to a division manager, 'Will you give me $100 million next year?' And they'd say, 'Oh, Mike, the economics of this and the housing starts, and this and that and the price of coffee in Brazil—there's no way I can get any more than $90.' And I'd say, 'Well, how about $95?' Then they'd say, 'Weeeelll, let me think about it for a couple of weeks.'

"We had become far too insular in our perspective," Bonsignore says. "We needed a whole new frame of reference against which to measure ourselves, inspire ourselves, challenge ourselves." So he and his staff identified Honeywell's chief competitors in every category—world-class names like General Electric, United Technologies, Allied Signal, Westinghouse, Rockwell, Tyco—and broke out their performance division by division. These numbers were then presented to each Honeywell division, which was informed: henceforth, these are the standards you will be living up to. If a Honeywell division came out in the bottom 25 percent when compared to its peers, then it was an underperformer. Period.

"All this created quite a bit of consternation," Bonsignore remarks dryly.

The new benchmarking system led to a second major change in operations: Honeywell would clearly distinguish between strategy and tactics. That is, overall financial planning would take place at the corporate level, instead of emerging from the business units. But responsibility and

authority for meeting the goals set at headquarters belonged to each business unit.

"Basically what we said in corporate headquarters was:
'*We* will set the targets and *you* will tell us how you're
gonna achieve the targets."

"Well," Bonsignore chuckles, "you could hear this gasp
all over the corporation: 'God, these people are wild men.
Look at what they're doing. They're *wild men.*'" All of a
sudden, a certain portion of Honeywell managers, who had
been guaranteeing themselves bonuses by lowballing performance goals, had just had the rug pulled out from under
them.

The revamped procedures were devised in 1993 and put
into practice the next year, Bonsignore's first full year as
CEO. They set the new tone: micromanaging and internal
squabbling were things of the past. In the new Honeywell,
certain things *must* be done, but only by those whose job it
was to do them. There would be accountability for failure.

The effect was to begin for the first time in corporate
memory to free division leaders to do their jobs, free of outside interference, but with clear objectives. Similarly, corporate staff people were able to stop wasting time and
energy pretending to know how each division ought to be
running day to day. "The management team, in retrospect,
breathed a giant sigh of relief because their energies were
not being sapped," says Bonsignore. "It's like the old bull
moose chasing his suitors away, and he gets so damned
tired chasing all his suitors away he never has any time left
for the lady. To some degree I felt the same in our case:
We spent so much time chasing each other around that

we didn't have any time left over to give to the business."

Bonsignore recognized, however, that poor company morale and a lack of competitive drive could not be addressed simply by devising new procedures. He needed a goal that everyone in the company could point toward. He began talking to his top staffers about an ambitious series of top-line growth goals, the headliner being that Honeywell would reach $10 billion in annual revenue by the year 2000. This was a remarkable goal for a company that hadn't budged much above $6 billion in a decade.

"He took a lot of hassles on that," recalls Grayson. The discussions played out over a couple of months, and one top manager—a key finance executive who oversaw external growth—tried to rally others in corporate against the plan. "He was absolutely convinced that we were all crazy for setting the financial targets we had," says Grayson. "And he was an incredibly smart man. He was absolutely convinced that this was the dumbest thing that anybody could possibly do. He thought that was the death note. He threw himself in front of it and said, 'Don't do it, it's crazy. It's absolutely crazy.' "

The classic old-Honeywell form of resistance sprang up, an office-to-office lobbying campaign that created a small anti-benchmark faction, which began informally to lobby Bonsignore. There was no dramatic showdown; Bonsignore invariably and politely heard out his detractors, but always ended the conversation by assuring them that he was moving ahead. It was all quiet and genteel, but those in the executive suites knew they were watching a challenge to the new regime—and the demise of that challenge. "Mike just didn't cave in," Grayson says.

Looking back, Bonsignore says he simply saw no alternative. "I wanted to send a very strong signal to the organization. We were gonna do something different or die trying."

By February 1995, when the financial press began writing Bonsignore's obituary, "die trying" looked like a real possibility. "This is part of my job that I knew would be there," he remembers telling his wife at around that time, "but man oh man. I mean, things just can't get any worse. They *cannot get any worse.*" In fact, the twin beatings from the Street and the press set the stage for the defining moment in Bonsignore's tenure.

February was also the month of Honeywell's annual whip-up-the-troops management meeting at the Rancho Bernando Inn in San Diego. "There was some real concern as to how Mike was going to react to all of this," says Stranghoener.

Several days before the corporate staff headed for California, Bonsignore sat down in his conference room with chief operating officer Larry Moore and then-CFO Bill Hjerpee, and announced that he intended to respond to the run of bad publicity. He would give the assembled Honeywell managers "a challenge," something that would raise the stakes and put everyone's future on the line. Wall Street wasn't impressed with his forecast of $2.40 a share earnings for 1995? Fine. He would challenge his own troops to beat that by at least a dime, by growing 15 percent in 1996 and another 15 percent in 1997.

Senior management retreats are indulged in by most

large businesses, and in many cases "indulged" is the right word. The executive ranks spend some time golfing, getting a tan, drinking and eating a little too much and listening to the presentations that have been written for the company's top people. Humor interspersed with loftiness, or vice versa, are the order of the day.

Historically, this was pretty much the case at Honeywell, where every February ninety or so senior executives from around the world would spend three days following the same routine they had always followed, before heading back to work having had, presumably, a pleasant time bonding with their colleagues. But this was not to be like other years. Recalling that meeting, his first as CEO, Bonsignore says that, for him, the bottom line was, "If we didn't do something different, we were history. We were just history. I said, 'Gee, I don't want to be the guy who's on watch when Honeywell gets taken over. After *a hundred years*?' "

Several people who were in attendance recall that the mood of the group arriving in San Diego that year was anxious. "People were apprehensive about what Mike would say," Stranghoener recalls. "Mike was an untested CEO at the time—nobody knew what to expect. Some people were concerned that we wouldn't take the performance issues raised by *Barron's* and *Business Week* seriously enough. Others were hoping we wouldn't overreact to their criticisms and that things would be pretty much business as usual. There was no consensus, just an air of apprehension."

Bonsignore, who enjoys the genetic good fortune of good looks and a physically imposing frame, certainly *looks* like he's in charge when he mounts a podium, but in the unsettled circumstances, it was what he said more than how he looked that captured the audience's attention and imagination.

In his San Diego address, Bonsignore acknowledged what the critics were saying. "Honeywell is far from reaching its financial potential, and perhaps a different, motivated management team of outsiders could get the job done," he said. "I consider this a challenge that we must meet to prove these doubters wrong—take-the-gloves-off time! We must get off the defensive, and there is only one way: performance.

"With this in mind," he continued, "I offer you the San Diego Challenge," and he proceeded to lay out the numbers that would, if all went well, push the stock from the low thirties into the forties by 1997.

"This past month has been a very tough one for me personally," he said. "I am, after all, your representative in front of all our publics, and I haven't done you proud lately. What has kept me going was my confidence that we really are on the doorstep of a performance breakout. And *if* we make up our minds to do it, *it will happen.*" Failure, he added, would mean "early retirement for the senior management. I don't want to go diving that badly."

No Honeywell CEO in history had ever spoken as personally and as openly as Bonsignore did in his speech, and the crowd, tentative at first, was smiling and applauding by the end.

"He came out swinging," says Stranghoener. "For him to come across as strongly as he did at that time must have been very difficult, because he was under this tremendous amount of pressure. It was really the first time when Mike gave us these expectations that were clearly above the norm, and convinced people not only that we *must* do it but that we *could* do it. I think that was the start of a cultural shift in this company."

But it was only a beginning, and a tentative one at that. At the end of the evening, and for many days afterward, Honeywell's managers—those who had been present at Bonsignore's speech and the much larger number who heard about it later—talked about the numbers and the vision their CEO had put before them. And the dominant note in those conversations was of anxiety that the company really couldn't do much better than it had been doing. There just wasn't much confidence that Honeywell could pick up the gauntlet its aggressive new leader had thrown down.

There were other concerns, as well. Gayle Pincus, the Phoenix industrial control manager, attended the conference and gives a different perspective on Bonsignore's address, that of a seasoned corporate manager who has seen programs come and go. When the glow of the moment faded, she says, she wondered if Bonsignore's speech would turn out to be "just more talk." But in the months following San Diego, Pincus was surprised to see real change taking shape—smart acquisitions, major departures in divisional operating procedures. "It wasn't until the changes came about," she says, "that people could actually imagine achieving those goals."

"I used to stop employees in the hall and say, 'What are we here for? What's our purpose?' " Bonsignore says. The answer he usually got was, " 'All I know is I'm running ninety miles an hour and I have no idea where I'm going.' In many ways I felt this myself."

What Bonsignore saw was an almost spiritual crisis. It was clear that simple strategic goals—based on numbers and charts—weren't enough. The company's workforce of dispirited clock-punchers had to be rejuvenated, given a reason to believe that they were part of a winner worthy of commitment. James Porter, whom Bonsignore tapped as vice president of human resources, was charged with canvassing a cross-section of Honeywell employees— ultimately some two thousand of them—and helping Bonsignore find a language in which to couch his vision of the future. "Out of this," says Bonsignore, "came this very simple vision: delighted customers, profitable growth and leadership in control.

"It sounded . . . so *elementary*. So sophomoric when we put it together. We thought, 'They're gonna think we're a bunch of jerks,' " he says, laughing. But Porter, among others, insisted that he stick with these simple propositions. If he came back to them in every communication with employees, and didn't let them fade away—if he stayed "on message," as it were—it would start to make a difference. "People have to hear it a few times before they can get past their skepticism and really start to think you mean it," Porter observed.

They heard it more than a few times. Throughout 1994, Bonsignore relentlessly engaged his people through every available channel. New voice mail and E-mail systems made it possible for him to communicate with workers throughout the company; videotaped presentations were mailed out; Bonsignore had his license plates changed to D LITEM. And he spent a startling one-third of his schedule with employees, making time for Q&A sessions with employees every time he visited a Honeywell facility.

The whole point was to make *himself* present to and known to his people, in a manner utterly foreign to the tradition of his office. They had to see him as someone passionately committed to the pursuit of a higher level of achievement. At first, Honeywell managers doubted Bonsignore was serious. For example, in 1994 he invited himself to a home and industrial control awards ceremony for the unit's top sales people, but never received details until after the ceremony was over. "Finally I got hold of the [division] president and he said, 'Well, people didn't think you were serious.'

" 'What do you mean people didn't think I was serious?'

" 'Well,' " Bonsignore recalls the manager's answer, " 'in the history of those things no CEO's ever gone, and they didn't think you were serious about flying down to Orlando, Florida, to spend an afternoon with those people.'

"I was *dead* serious about it," Bonsignore says emphatically. "So when it came around again in '95 I went. And I was down again a couple of weeks ago. Flew into Orlando at nine o'clock at night, got up the next morning, gave out fifty awards, got on a plane and flew away. But people will *remember* that, *talk* about that."

And slowly, it started to work. "When he got in front of groups of people, regardless of what kinds of people, whether they were finance people, internal, or outside the company, or people on our board, he was saying the same things to them that he would say to me," Porter says.

"That's really a clear indicator of what's important to people: when they talk about things that aren't necessarily geared toward the audience that they're speaking to. He was consistent."

Gradually, Bonsignore began to get clear answers to his random questions about what the company stood for. When he got questions back, they were framed by the issues he'd set forth: What are new ways we can delight customers instead of just satisfying them? Is this new project going to help us grow profitably? How are we doing against this competitor, and what does that securities analyst think of us now? When employees had complaints, they signed their letters, a sure sign of trust. And Bonsignore made his E-mail address public so employees could zap their concerns to him directly. Nor was this access abused. "I probably get ten [such] E-mails a week," he says. "About half are [about something] they think we can do better. The other half are telling me about something that's really exciting . . . that I ought to call so and so and congratulate them about a contract."

In 1995, Bonsignore sat down with communications and human relations executives from around the company, to see what their focus groups and employee surveys were telling them about his campaign. "I said, 'Okay, I want to know how the employees are feeling about the vision, because frankly, it sounds so elementary.' " He laughs. "And I am telling you, they came back with a vengeance and said, 'If you change that thing you're *dead meat.*' They were *really* that adamant about it: Whatever you do, *don't change it.*" In 1996 and 1997, the message was the same.

As Bonsignore puts it, his marathon campaign to spread

the gospel of the new Honeywell allowed him to be seen, and ultimately trusted, as "a person, just a person. Not an executive or a CEO, but just a person, and [as] comfortable talking with the maintenance crew here as talking with my policy committee." He wanted his employees to follow him, and he wanted them to know why. It was as drastic a break with the company's history as anything he did.

"I don't know that this would ever win a prize in the Harvard Business School," he says. "But it seems to work." And the people in the hallway now know why they are there.

To bolster his internal relations campaign, Bonsignore also boosted his company's real-dollar investments in its own people. "One of the first things we did when we came into this job," Porter says, "was to try to get a baseline for what we were really investing as a corporation in training the people. We really didn't know." It was a remarkable state of affairs for a major corporation in the mid-1990s.

So human resources managers in every business unit were forced—"kicking and screaming," Porter notes—to explain what they were doing to train their people and how much they were spending in exact dollar amounts. "All around the world, they hated us for a while," Porter says. "But we basically told 'em, 'We don't know, we've got to have a basis, we've got to understand what our investment level is. And we need to understand what the quality of our training and development processes are. We need to know, first of all, how much are we spending on this? Are we getting any kind of return at all?' " Porter assigned someone from corporate training and development who spent eight months developing a clear picture of Honeywell's commitment to its people.

Porter, meanwhile, rounded up similar numbers from world-class companies like Hewlett-Packard, Motorola, IBM, Microsoft, and soon found they were way ahead of Honeywell in making and tracking such investments. They set aside, on average, 3.5 to 4.5 percent of payroll for training, versus just 1.6 percent at Honeywell in 1993. This provoked a clear message from Minneapolis that further training cuts (a popular target for hitting short-term profit goals) were verboten. In fact, such spending was to be increased to meet Honeywell's long-term growth goals. A target was set—4 percent of payroll—and by the end of 1996 the company had nearly doubled its investment to 2.9 percent.

Part of this increase, in the form of the "Explore" program, was focused on low-level and potential supervisors. It gave them a chance to "pre-train" for supervisory positions, enhancing their chances for promotion, and shortening the learning curve when it happened.

Beyond that, the learning programs focused on two themes: leadership and change. Honeywell launched what it calls the "Change Capability Project," which began by identifying thirty "change champions" within the company, who draw on their own experiences to create a model that managers company-wide can use to understand the need for change and ways to encourage it. Executives can also nominate top-performing managers for four-week intensive management courses at the company's Leadership Institute in Minnesota. (Indeed, they are forced to make such nominations—Bonsignore says he has personally intervened when business heads have tried to dodge sending someone to the Institute as a way to trim expenses.) Through this last project alone, Honeywell managers now absorb almost forty thousand classroom hours in training every year.

In May 1995, Jennifer Pokrzywinski, an analyst with Morgan Stanley, had some good things and some bad things to say about Honeywell stock. On the plus side, the company had "three tremendous global franchises. Businesses with these types of market shares and global presence should earn superior financial returns," she said. General Electric had done it. Emerson Electric had done it. "In contrast," she continued, "the experience with Honeywell has been one of more negative surprises. The company has spent a lot of money on a lot of restructuring in the past five and even ten years. We have yet to see any real payoff from that restructuring. Financial returns remain mediocre, and this is really a mystery and a frustration to Honeywell shareholders.

"I don't sense that there is a widespread awareness at Honeywell of financial returns or of shareholder value," she summed up. "I would like to recommend Honeywell stock, and the day that I do sense that awareness is the day that I'll recommend the stock."

That's the kind of analysis most managers would just as soon their employees didn't hear. But these comments were part of a videotaped presentation on the subject of creating value that was distributed all over Honeywell to bring employees face-to-face with what Bonsignore calls "the bogeyman shareholder."

Michael R. Robinson, Honeywell's former vice president of investor relations helped put together the video. He also arranged for analysts and shareholders to speak in person to groups of managers. "It was clearly an eye-opener," he says. "When they can hear it from the horse's mouth, it takes away a lot of the skepticism, a lot of the 'Hey, I'm doing my best.' Which was the internal culture. There had always been a disconnect between the employee, the manager, who works for the company, and the shareholder," he says. "Generally, I don't know that an employee knew who or what a shareholder was, and what the expectations were."

Still, understanding shareholder concerns is hardly the same as *owning* stock in a company and watching your wallet wax and wane with its price. "I can remember when I first started talking about shareholder value creation when I took over. I could tell when I talked to a group of employees that in most cases, they tuned me out completely," Bonsignore says. "For them, 'shareholder' was synonymous with someone who made their life miserable: some group off in New York that wanted more and more and more, and they didn't understand our problem, and they were a thorn in our side. I knew I would never win this battle until I could make employee and shareholder one."

The answer, clearly, was to go ahead and, as Captain Jean-Luc Picard might say, "Make it so." A major program was instituted to increase employee ownership of Honeywell stock, either through the 401(k) plan or direct purchase. In 1993, about 3 percent of Honeywell stock was owned by employees. By 1997, that percentage had doubled, making Honeywell employees the company's largest single shareholder group. Eighty percent of U.S. workers are now shareholders and the company is currently reaching out to its twenty thousand employees outside the United States in hopes of pushing the percentage of Honeywell stock owned by employees up to 15 percent.

Similarly, in 1993, only about 15 percent of the Honeywell's U.S. workforce was on some kind of variable pay plan, notes Porter. Implementation of new profit-sharing, incentive, and bonus schemes increased that to 70 percent by 1997. "If Honeywell does well financially, our employees are sharing in the rewards that come with that," Porter says. These real-world changes have dovetailed with the education effort. Now, Robinson says, when he arrives in Honeywell operations all over the world to give value-creation talks, he's frequently asked, "What about that Jennifer Pokrzywinski—what does she think of us today?' " (As of June 1998, she had a hold recommendation on the company.) And Porter recalls a startled former CFO fielding detailed questions from a machine operator in Albuquerque about the high working capital of a Honeywell plant in Golden Valley, Minnesota. "That's having an impact on my paycheck here. I'd like to know what they're doing about it," demanded the line worker.

Or consider what happened at a Honeywell space and aviation unit in Phoenix. After sitting through a new course on business basics, a group of machine operators began talking as they walked out of the classroom. The plant operated on two shifts, with several hours separating them. But because the machinery took over an hour to warm up, it was left running all night—after the second shift—so it would be ready when the morning shift arrived. The operators, says Porter, "decided that it was not acceptable to use that electricity and to increase the wear and tear on the machines. So on their own, they went out to some hardware stores, bought some timers and rigged them up." Now, the machines are shut down for four or five hours after the late shift, and timers turn them back on before the seven A.M. shift arrives. This saves money on electricity and by reducing required maintenance. It's an elegant, economical solution to a workplace problem that would never have been addressed at all without the training program, says Porter.

All of this is an exercise in corporate self-interest, of course, though one in which, theoretically, everybody wins. The whole point, says Bonsignore, is to "get to a point where they'll say, 'I'm making this decision in my work because it will be good for the company and that in turn will be good for me.' "

Nineteen-ninety-five, which had started so ominously for Bonsignore, would end triumphantly. Everything—the clear objectives, stringent benchmarks, and strict accountability that he had put in place in 1994—started to generate results. The company made good on the promises Wall Street had scoffed at in 1994 and exceeded the San Diego

Challenge. Honeywell had pledged earnings growth of 16 percent and had delivered 22 percent. It had promised first $2.40, and then $2.50 a share, and it had delivered $2.62 a share. Sales, net, return on equity—by every measure, Honeywell exceeded expectations. The successes cut across Honeywell's three primary business units, but in particular, avionics scored a major coup by delivering a new navigational system for Boeing's new 777 line of jets, and industrial was reworking its relationships with major clients like Phillips and Amoco to assume total responsibility for control in major power and refining operations.

With his in-house engine humming, Bonsignore began to look outside for ways to augment growth and profitability. One of the benefits of previous restructuring was that Honeywell's debt was under control and its cash flow relatively strong, so he decided to move ahead with an acquisition program. "And as soon as I mention the word acquisition everybody runs for the foxholes," he recalls. "We'd had a disastrous acquisition history at Honeywell. So, obviously, the management team was pretty spooked."

Bonsignore was determined, however, to do things differently this time around. He emphasized two things. First, the acquisitions would be small and strategic. Second, and critically, ideas for acquisitions would come from the business divisions, not corporate. As Bonsignore puts it, "From day one I had said: 'The ideas for acquisitions will not come out of this office.' That's where we made the big mistake last time. A CEO would say, 'We really ought to be in the medical business because it's growing.' 'Well, okay, but what do we know about medical?' 'Don't worry about that, just get into the medical business.' Management saw these as opportunities to grow, but didn't spend enough time asking the questions: What do we bring to these businesses? What do semiconductors and medical electronics and communications service have to do with each other? Well, really, nothing; they're just fast-growing markets. And we had convinced ourselves we ought to be in 'em."

So he set the rules: strategic fit, a strong risk-adjusted return, tough due-diligence. Then he got the word out and waited for the business units to respond. It took about a year and a half, he estimates, before things started to click. The acquisitions weren't headline-grabbers, but they made sense. To take one minor example: The company's home and building control team in Europe had been watching Satronic, a Swiss boiler manufacturer for years. They made their case to corporate, Bonsignore liked it, and Honeywell gobbled up Satronic in 1996 for $41 million; it added $36 million to revenue that year, a figure projected to grow rapidly through the end of the century.

"Now, lo and behold, we've made something like thirty-odd acquisitions over the last three years," Bonsignore says, "and they have been far above the average in terms of probability of success, because we kept the focus very much on what we know how to do." In all, the company had completed sixty-three acquisitions on Bonsignore's watch as of mid-1998, for a total of about $1.2 billion. Those acquisitions have already added at least that much to sales as of 1998, and should add more going forward.

A more dramatic example of Honeywell's new acquisition strategy had its origins in the domestic home and business control division. During the company's annual strategic planning process, the company evaluated each of the traditional distribution channels for its home and buildings business: distributors, contractors, builders, and so on. The Honeywell tradition, Bonsignore said, was, 'We will always sell to the consumer through somebody else. That's the way we do it. The consumer doesn't know us.'

"Somewhere along the way we said, 'Stop—how do we know the consumer doesn't know us?' " So Honeywell retained a marketing research firm, which concluded that, partly because its thermostats were in practically every house in America, Honeywell's brand recognition was astoundingly high. Bonsignore remembers the firm's report with some amusement. "They said, 'This is the most remarkable reaction we've ever gotten. The consumer gives you guys credit for a lot of things you don't even do. You're the number two air conditioner manufacturer, you're in kitchen appliances.' And I'll never forget the cover letter from the guy that did this study. He said, 'My advice to you is run, don't walk, into the consumer business.' "

Then along came Duracraft, a maker of heaters, humidifiers, vaporizers and the like. In other words, a consumer company in the business of home comfort control. Brian McGourty, then the head of home and building control, convinced Bonsignore and the top executives in Minneapolis that this was the perfect fit. They bought Duracraft for $283 million in early 1996, and later that year Honeywell-branded products began to appear in retailers like Sears, Target, Wal-Mart and Home Depot. And they flew off the shelves. "It's blown open a channel for us in retail which, in 1997, amounted to four hundred million dollars in sales," Bonsignore says. "Four hundred million dollars in sales!

"For me, Duracraft has been the most remarkable thing because we did something that no one at Honeywell had ever thought of before. We refined the strategic planning process to the point where a question like 'What do you mean we don't have any consumer identity?' could get asked, without some conventional thinking in the company batting it down as a stupid question."

By early 1997, no one on Wall Street was laughing at Honeywell or Michael Bonsignore anymore. Total sales for 1996 were $7.31 billion, up from about $6 billion in 1994. Net income was $403 million, up from $279 in '94. Earnings per share: up to $3.18 from $2.15 in '94. The share price was in the 70s, up from 27 in '94. Two years to the month after its bruising cover story, *Barron's* ran a brief article titled, "Unlocking the Wealth: Honeywell lives up to its name with sweet earnings growth." Bonsignore told the magazine he expected sales growth in the 8 to 10 percent range, and 1 to 1.5 percent yearly improvements on margins; he pegged 1997 earnings per share at $3.68, and $4.22 in 1998. This time around, they skipped the cartoon.

By the close of fiscal 1997, Bonsignore had delivered on his promises. In fact, full-year earnings for 1997 were $3.71 per share, and for the first time ever, Honeywell topped $8 billion in sales, a 10 percent increase from 1996. And as performance has improved, Bonsignore's star has risen in the media and within the investment community. Wall

Street likes the stock again, and the CEO regularly makes trips to New York to appear on *Moneyline,* CNN, Fox and Bloomberg, spreading the good news—another communications task his predecessors had shown little interest in.

It may be a real-life fairy tale, but in the end, did Bonsignore truly work magic? He says no. Honeywell had the pieces for success in place, and, he contends, he happens to have been the person with the right "skill set" at the right time. "If I had not had good communication skills and good interpersonal skills, I don't think we would have made the progress we've made," he says. "The board of directors knew what kind of skills they needed—not an autocratic 'Here's what we think at corporate' style. They knew that we had to get these people on board emotionally, on board with their hearts and minds."

On the other hand, Bonsignore notes, as a longtime Honeywell employee, he's learned a great deal about what he calls "generational changes" in the nature of corporate leadership. "I was really struck by the contrast between the tear-it-down stage of evolution and the build-it-up stage— what was required for each," he says. "I would have been a dismal failure if I had had to tear the company apart. I could have done it, but I would have been so miserable personally that I probably would not have stayed. I would've left."

What's more, the nature of corporate leadership continues to change, more quickly than ever. Bonsignore figures that the days of a single individual running a Honeywell-size company for fifteen or twenty years are fading. "I think today a CEO who's in a job for more than ten years has really got to be an extraordinary individual," he observes. To that end, Bonsignore is already starting up the process that will lead to the selection of his successor. "Believe me there will come a time—and I think the time comes sooner rather than later today—when I am gonna be the dinosaur," he says. "Somebody's gonna have to recognize it. I hope the first person that's gonna recognize it will be me."

7/Leon Hirsch
Letting Go

At an age when most CEOs are less worried about business than putting, seventy-one-year-old Leon Hirsch has just started a new job. On June 1, 1998, Hirsch agreed to sell U.S. Surgical Corp., the Connecticut-based medical technology company he founded forty years ago in his basement and literally with his own hands. The price was $3.9 billion and the buyer was Tyco International, an acquisitive $15 billion-a-year conglomerate with a burgeoning medical products group.

The deal makes sense. Tyco gets U.S. Surgical's world-class products and sales force, and it gets Hirsch to run the medical products division. In return, U.S. Surgical will gain the marketing muscle and broad product line it needs to level the playing field with giant Johnson & Johnson Corp., its chief competitor. The merger will ensure the future of U.S.S.

In fact, the deal makes such good sense that the only surprise, perhaps, is that Leon Hirsch was willing to do it. Despite his ruddy face, silver hair and impish smile, Hirsch is a fiercely combative and independent executive, and the preeminent medical entrepreneur of the post–World War II era. He is, moreover, a man with neither a medical degree nor a college diploma, who nevertheless was accepted into the exclusive medical fraternity, and revolutionized how it practiced surgery.

For many years, U.S. Surgical was his company, the sort of place that never had a layoff and where Hirsch addressed the entire company each year, personally answering any question any employee had. To this day, a visit to company headquarters in Norwalk, Connecticut, is likely to include an unsolicited testimonial to "Mr. Hirsch" from any security guard or secretary who finds you wandering the halls.

Unfortunately, it's just such proprietary ownership, a hallmark of many successful start-ups, which often presages disaster as a company matures. In fact, entrepreneurs generally make lousy CEOs. The problem is they love their companies—often, to death. For in the end, the hardest thing an entrepreneur has to do may not be to succeed, but to let others succeed. His or her company, at some point, must make it possible for others to consider it their company too. Selling U.S.S. was only the most recent evidence that Hirsch had learned this difficult lesson. And he did so when it counted most, when the very survival of his company was at stake.

Hirsch was born in 1927, one of three children, and raised on the fifth floor of a Bronx tenement. His father, a Polish émigré, and his mother ran a small neighborhood lingerie shop, which, even in the midst of the Great Depression, enabled the family to make ends meet. "It was called the Hub," Hirsch recalls. "It was a tough neighborhood—Italian, German, with a little bit of Irish. On Sundays, you would see the German fathers, ten or fifteen of them, working men, dressed in their Sunday suits, walking down the street, each carrying a pitcher of beer. They'd go down to the local bar, get a pitcher and walk home with it for Sunday dinner."

Later, when Hirsch was a teenager, the family moved to the Bronx's Grand Concourse, just blocks from Yankee Stadium. In that neighborhood, life—or at least a child's life—was dominated by the Yankee presence. Hirsch fondly remembers how all the neighborhood kids would head for the stadium in the late morning; a few of them would be picked to "turn stiles" (let in ticket holders), which they did until the third inning. Then they were paid a quarter and, wonder of wonders, got to watch the rest of the game free.

"Every day that I didn't turn stiles, as soon as I got home in the afternoon, I'd run up to the roof and look to see if the blue flag or the red flag was up," Hirsch says. "After the game, the Yankees always put up either the red or the blue flag with a white cross. Blue was for victory; red for defeat."

In school, Hirsch displayed an unusual aptitude for the sciences—and salesmanship. In fact, he was so adept at the latter that he convinced Morris Meister, the founding principal of New York City's legendary Bronx High School of Science, to admit him. despite the fact that he had failed the school's competitive entrance exam. Bronx Science, as it's called, was and is today a sort of meritocratic conveyor belt, moving the city's most ambitious kids on to first-rate scientific or technical educations—and taking them out of the neighborhood and into the great world. Thousands of young men and women have made the journey over the decades. But in 1945, when it came time for Hirsch to apply to college, he stunned everyone who knew him by enlisting in the Army Air Corps, just months before the dropping of the atom bomb. With the war winding down, Hirsch was mustered out after eighteen months, never having had to fight. But once again, instead of going to college (with the GI Bill to pay for it), he went to work.

"Meister was furious," Hirsch recalls, "and he never forgave me. In 1968 or 1969, when *Time* magazine wrote about U.S. Surgical and me, I sent a copy of the article to Meister, with a note which said, 'See, I did make something of myself.' He sent it back, writing on it in black ink, 'This doesn't count, you should still go to college.' "

Hirsch was one of only three people in his graduating class not to go on to higher education. "I just didn't want to go to school anymore," he says, looking back. "Maybe if I hadn't gone into the army I wouldn't have felt that way. I enjoyed the freedom I had there—it just gave me a great sense of freedom. So when I got out, I wanted to do the things I wanted to do. A high school education was all I felt I needed to get out into the world to start accomplishing things."

There was, of course, the question of money. "There was no way in hell I was going to do what my Mom and Pop did," Hirsch says. "I watched them work. On a Saturday they'd be in that store from ten in the morning to eleven at night. On a weekday they closed at nine o'clock. That was not going to be the life for me. Money was my passport out of [that] life."

As an additional spur, Hirsch, like all the other return-ing vets who kicked the baby boom generation into gear, married and quickly began a family.

Smart and willing to hustle, Hirsch figured, correctly, that there would be tremendous pent-up demand after the long wartime years of shortages and rationing of consumer products. He tried a number of ways to take advantage of it: He was a frozen food salesman and a hawker of storm windows and sewing machines. He was successful, though, insofar as he made a good living. But by his own estima-tion, he had still not "freed himself."

By 1963, the thirty-six-year-old Hirsch was running a failing coin-operated dry cleaning equipment manufactur-ing facility in Cincinnati ("A terrible business," he says with a grimace of remembrance). Looking for a more promising venture, he met with a Manhattan business broker, and while they were talking he found himself playing with a curious piece of equipment on the man's desk. When told that it was a Russian surgical stapler, Hirsch asked the ob-vious question: "What's that?"

The answer was that the device was supposed to allow surgeons to staple, rather than stitch, people together. A Russian trade organization had asked the broker to sell the stapler in the United States, but, Hirsch recalled, "He'd gone to all the medical device manufacturers, and they'd all laughed at him. Their reaction was the same as mine. I thought it was the stupidest thing I'd ever heard of. But he gave me a marketing manual and told me to read it. I didn't understand a word of it but the book named three American surgeons who visited Russia as part of an exchange program."

Hirsch called Dr. Mark Ravitch at Johns Hopkins University Medical School, one of those visiting surgeons. Ravitch said that the idea of stapling patients had tremendous potential advantages over sewing them up. It could halve operating times, dramatically reducing patient trauma, blood loss and convalescent periods. However, the Russian device was not the answer, the doctor said. It was far too cumbersome and virtually impossible to load.

"He showed me how they loaded this Russian surgical stapler," Hirsch remembers. "They took a petri dish and put all these teensy little staples in it and autoclave it, and then the nurse is supposed to stand there and use a tweezers to load them one at a time. Aside from the fact that she would never do it, it was dangerous. You could miss one, you could bend one." Nonetheless, Hirsch was intrigued by the gadget's possibilities, and Ravitch agreed to let him borrow one.

Back home, tinkering alone in his basement, Hirsch came up with an ingenious solution: Put the staples in a cartridge, just the way disposable razor blades are packaged and held ready for insertion into a razor. In less than a week, he recalls, "I cobbled a cartridge up out of balsa wood, I loaded up the staples, I took it back to [Ravitch] and asked him what he thought. He got very excited. 'That's easy!' he told me. 'Anybody could do that.'

"Mark Ravitch said to me, 'I'll work with you on this. All I want is the right to publish. I don't want any money because if you pay me anything I won't be able to be objective. But I also have to tell you that if I don't like it I'm going to say it's dangerous and I'm going to publish that.' "

Ravitch, along with a colleague, agreed to test a working model, so Hirsch spent all his savings, about $75,000, building metal prototypes. While the two doctors tested the device, yet another surgeon Hirsch had met showed the balsa model to Zanvyl Krieger, at the time a principal owner of the Baltimore Orioles. By this time, Ravitch had used the device successfully in several operations and was sufficiently enthusiastic that Krieger and another investor, Ben Rosenbloom, put up $2 million for two-thirds of the fledgling company, with Hirsch keeping the remaining third.

It took Hirsch from 1964 until 1967 to perfect the stapler and to get the tooling done for mass production. Figuring out how to automate loading the tiny surgical staples (each the diameter of two human hairs) into cartridges without bending them proved fiendishly difficult. In 1967, too, the fledgling company floated its initial public offering, selling both common and convertible stock, raising $400,000 (the common went for just $.32 a share). When the company finally went into business, however, a serious problem immediately raised its head.

Surgeons, who tend to like gadgets, were happy to tell their hospitals to go out and buy the stapler, but they showed much less interest in learning to use it. So the stapler would sit on the shelf, which meant the supplies of staples never got used up. And since all the profits were to come from selling additional cartridges (again, precisely the same business model employed by the big razor blade companies), U.S.S. was quickly going broke. Hirsch recalls, "In

1968, our first full year of operation, we had about $380,000 in revenues but we lost $400,000. We discovered that the problem was not selling, but education."

Hirsch's assistant (who later became his second wife) Turi Josefsen came up with a solution. Neither a doctor nor a nurse, she had begun assisting surgeons who were working with U.S. Surgical's prototype stapler. She proved to have "good hands" in their opinion, and quickly became an uncredentialed surgical assistant. Turi decided to put her new skills to work. She went and scrubbed with the surgeons, then taught them how to use the staplers right in the operating chamber. After a few operations, the surgeons, grown comfortable with the technology, were hooked. Following the success of this pilot program, Josefsen hired eleven registered nurses and trained them for two weeks in the use of the stapler. Then, she dispatched them to hospital operating rooms around the country. This worked, too, but nurses are not salespeople and Hirsch needed sales. So, about a year later, he and Josefsen did something truly audacious: Offering generous commissions, they began hiring salesmen who would work right alongside the surgeon. (The initial interviews took place in an office with a movie projector running films of surgical procedures on one wall. Interviewees who suddenly looked ill were politely excused.)

Fifteen men were in the first group. They were all nonmedical people, who had sold IBM typewriters, Xerox copiers, real estate, insurance and the like—and they were put through a six-day-a-week, six-week medical boot camp. They were taught basic anatomy, physiology, terminology, instrumentation, surgical protocols, and fifty different procedures using the stapler. Most important, they were taught how to talk surgeons through a procedure so that they became comfortable using the stapler in the operating chamber. Then they were told to hit the road, as the company's first Auto Suture Co. Certified Stapling Technicians.

Hirsch was relentless. He gave his sales force huge quotas, and there was no excuse for falling short. In truth, he had no choice. His company was losing money every year, and some of his investors were growing more than restive. Indeed, in 1969, one senior manager at Donaldson Lufkin & Jenrette, the New York investment bankers, said he'd had enough and would pour no more funds into U.S.S. It was time, he said, to sell the company or shut it down.

Hirsch went on the offensive, just as he had when Morris Meister had rejected him from Bronx Science. He insisted on a face-to-face meeting with Dan Lufkin, to which he took Zanvyl Krieger, one of his principal investors. At the meeting, Hirsch recalls, the DLJ manager repeated his intention of selling the company, to which Lufkin responded, "To whom? For what?" After all, there was hardly a robust market for a money-losing manufacturer of an exotic surgical instrument. Instead, Lufkin himself proposed to Krieger that they should personally invest $150,000 each, in exchange for stock. Krieger agreed.

That $300,000 bought Hirsch the time he needed. In 1970, U.S. Surgical made a $52,000 profit on sales of just under one-and-a-half million dollars. Two years later, revenue exceeded $5 million, and profits had risen sixfold. By 1974, U.S.S. had reached nearly $13 million in sales, and $1.5 million in net income. Four years after that, those numbers had climbed to $40,639,000 and $3,660,000, respectively.

By 1983, U.S. Surgical had reached $160 million in annual sales. In fact, it had no real competitors. Johnson & Johnson, the biggest suture maker, showed little interest, Hirsch recalls gratefully. J&J's attitude on staples was that it was a big yawn, he says. "That was very fortunate for us, because they could have put us out of business very easily in the 1970s."

You couldn't have told from watching Hirsch that J&J, or some other medical behemoth, wasn't breathing down his company's neck, as the business world at large became aware after *The New York Times* published an extensive article on U.S.S. in 1984. The *Times* described Hirsch as being nearly unbalanced by "a hunger for growth, a hunger that apparently gnawed at [him]." He put so much pressure on his sales people, the *Times* charged, that some of them resorted to stealing U.S. Surgical products from hospitals so they would be forced to reorder more quickly. In one case, a sales manager said that a hospital ceiling had collapsed because a huge excess quantity of staples had been stockpiled in the storeroom above. And a former regional sales manager stated flatly, "The company has absolutely no ethics from a sales point."

Hirsch, who grew up playing stickball on the streets of the Bronx, was never one to back away from a good fight. He vigorously counterattacked, calling the *Times*'s article a "hatchet job," and adding, "The article reports as truths unproven allegations which became the basis of a 1982 SEC investigation against the company." Hirsch and other senior U.S.S. executives suspect that investigation was prompted by a former sales director, whose request to set up a U.S.S. subsidiary in Australia was refused.

Says Hirsch, "He ultimately went to Australia anyway, reverse engineered our products, got Australian patents and started a competing business, which he sold to a well-known U.S. company. We took him to court and won a $73.5 million judgment, which we're still trying to collect, since we have been unable to locate him.

"The *Times* article also does not report that the salesperson who told the story of the collapsed ceiling was investigated by the company and fired well before that incident was made public."

■

Still, the 1982 SEC investigation concluded, among other things, that the company had used improper accounting to inflate earnings. It found that in 1981, when U.S. Surgical reported pretax income of $12.9 million, the company had actually made just $200,000. And for the years 1979–1982, the company agreed to settle its differences with the SEC by lowering its earnings by a total of $26 million. Hirsch himself had to repay a bonus of more than $317,000.

To this day, Hirsch resolutely denies any wrongdoing by his employees or by himself, and notes that the SEC never asked that a single U.S.S. employee be fired as part of the settlement the company reached with the government. The charges of accounting improprieties, he contends, were never about actual dollar amounts, but only about the way U.S.S. timed its reporting of sales and expenses. "Certain sales were shifted to later periods," he says, "and the reporting of certain expenses was accelerated." Still, to avoid years of litigation and ongoing negative publicity, U.S.S. settled all the SEC's charges, though in a manner that the company's accounting firm advised did not compromise the company's assertion of innocence. As part of the deal, U.S. Surgical agreed to institute stricter internal controls and to create an internal audit department.

Whatever the ultimate legal merits of the SEC's case, however, it's fair to say that U.S. Surgical's reputation was not enhanced by the investigation or *The New York Times* article, and that it was hardly regarded as a model corporate citizen. And when people looked to point a finger of blame, they pointed at Leon Hirsch. As a former employee told the *Times,* "The problem [with U.S.S.] was Leon Hirsch's insatiable appetite for success."

But despite the occasional stumble, for nearly twenty years starting in 1970, U.S. Surgical grew at a dizzying 34 percent compounded annual rate, to $345 million twenty years later, in 1989. The company soon began to attract the notice of the financial press, and Hirsch himself, who had little patience with courting the press or industry analysts, was not always treated kindly. *Forbes* magazine, for one, called him cocky, and the investment community, acknowledges Marianne Scipione, the long-time vice president of investor relations, saw him as a one-man band, at a company with no depth of management. Nor were they far wrong, according to Thomas Kuczenski, a former U.S.S. marketing analyst who is now a medical consultant. Hirsch made every decision, Kuczenski recalls. And for a long time, he seemed unable to make a bad one.

Then in 1988 U.S. Surgical introduced a new product at

the American College of Surgeons meeting that would profoundly change modern surgery. It was called an endoscopic clip applier, a cumbersome name for an elegant technology. It allowed physicians to do gallbladder surgery on an outpatient basis, with the patient up and about within a week. The applier worked in conjunction with a device called a trocar, which used a disposable blade to make a tiny incision in the belly, into which fiber optic lenses and miniaturized surgical instruments were inserted. Instead of coping with an eight-inch incision in the abdomen, a six-to-seven-day stay in the hospital, and six to eight weeks of recovery time, patients could resume normal activities in only a few days, and save thousands of dollars of medical costs in the bargain.

Hirsch and U.S.S. had once again revolutionized surgery. The explosion in endoscopic, or minimally invasive, surgery was under way, with the company at the forefront, forcing all its competitors to rapidly enter the endoscopic market with products of their own. Demand for clip appliers and trocars was so great that U.S. Surgical couldn't ship them fast enough. Says Hirsch, "The surgical community, which is normally very conservative, jumped on this." U.S. Surgical's one-thousand-strong global sales force fanned out to hospitals throughout the world, training them in the new technology and signing orders at a breakneck pace. From 1988 to 1992, endoscopic surgery vaulted U.S. Surgical to a record four straight years of extraordinary growth. Sales jumped to $1.2 billion and were growing at a 30 percent compounded annual rate. Earnings for 1992 hit $138 million, and were growing at a 60 percent compounded annual rate, while the company's stock climbed to $134 a share, a remarkable fifty-five times earnings.

Wall Street loved Hirsch's corporate baby. Lorraine Schwartz, an analyst with the brokerage house Wertheim Schroeder, called U.S. Surgical a "pound the table buy," and Paine Webber's David Lothson said that the company was still in a very, very rapid growth mode.

Those were heady times, and in fact the company was heading straight for disaster. "Our experience was that surgeons would adapt to endoscopic surgery slowly as they did to stapling," says Hirsch, "so we were expecting orders to grow in a steady fashion. We were unprepared for what happened. We were totally undersized. We got into terrific problems with production, quality and training. Our customers got very aggravated. We just couldn't deliver."

It never occurred to Hirsch to limit demand and grow at a steadier pace. Instead, he set the company on an ambitious plant expansion plan, spending nearly $300 million. That built the company's debt to $505 million—nearly 50 percent of revenues and 350 percent of net earnings. "Nine out of ten times our decision would have been the right one," says Hirsch. But not this time.

In 1992, just as additional production was coming on line, Hillary Rodham Clinton announced her healthcare initiative. Literally, almost to the day, says Hirsch, hospitals panicked. "Purchasing decisions were taken away from the surgeons and made by administrators on a cost basis rather than an efficacy basis, and the bottom fell out of our business. Where we had planned for a sales increase, we not only had a sales decrease, but [profit] margin pressure because of price."

All of U.S. Surgical's flaws reared up to grab it by the throat. Hospital administrators, who loathed the company's high-pressure salesmen, began refusing to see them, on the grounds that all buying would be henceforth done through large central purchasing companies. Utterly dependent on the surgeons with whom it had forged relationships over almost three decades, U.S. Surgical was suddenly cut off.

Hirsch admits that it took him too long to recognize the serious trouble into which U.S.S. had fallen. The company, he says, lost a full year before implementing the solution to U.S. Surgical's problem. As Robert Knarr, U.S. Surgical's executive vice president for sales and marketing, says, "We spent a fair amount of time fooling ourselves that things would turn around. I call that period the era of self-delusion."

Hirsch's first tentative steps only made things worse. For example, when U.S. Surgical finally began selling through distributors in 1993, it raised havoc with inventory. The company was accustomed to loading up hospitals with inventory, but the distributors demanded delivery on a just-in-time basis. As a result, inventory levels soared by more than $40 million in a single year, even as sales were beginning to fall. In 1993, sales dropped off by $60 million, and in 1994, by another $120 million. Between January 1992, when the stock hit 134, and February 1994, when it fell to $16, the company lost 88 percent of its market capitalization. "We had never been in a position of declining sales before," says Hirsch, and for a time he wasn't sure how to respond.

Wall Street began urging Hirsch to sell the company. Debt was huge, and because U.S. Surgical had been growing so fast, it had little cash in reserve to meet its losses (by the beginning of 1994, cash on hand and cash equivalents were down to $900,000). The company hemorrhaged market share to Johnson & Johnson, whose Ethicon division had belatedly entered U.S.S.'s market and was stealing away its customers by enticing hospital materials managers with extremely aggressive pricing.

Hirsch was sixty-seven, near or past the age of CEO retirement at most companies. Moreover, he and his wife Turi Josefsen were sued by shareholders for having cashed in on $120 million in options while the stock was near its high-water mark. (The shareholders alleged the two had known that the company was headed for a downturn. The suit was later settled out of court.) That, plus the lack of any heir apparent, and an empty till, set Wall Street to thinking how much fee income could be generated by merging the company with Boston Scientific or Medtronic, two fast-growing medical device companies.

Hirsch, however, was nothing if not a survivor, and he had no intention of walking away. It would have been tantamount to abandoning his child. Nonetheless, the time had come for decisive action and he needed his management team to buy into a plan of pain and sacrifice. The idea was to cut expenses drastically, raise money in the capital market (additional debt was not an option) and convince the banks that, if they kept their lines of credit open, U.S.S. would right itself. In the search for capital, Hirsch first went to an investment banker who introduced him to Jack Welch, General Electric's CEO. Hirsch asked Welch to buy 20 percent of U.S. Surgical. The overture failed, but, ironically, significantly aided the company in its efforts to save itself. As Hirsch says, "We were working internally on cost-cutting, but we didn't really understand anything about it. It was something we'd never done. With us it was always, 'You need more money? Okay, sell some more.' And it worked.

"Welch sent his people, including the treasurer and the chief financial officer, in to do due diligence and they really gave us a lesson in how to cut costs."

The end result was a 1993 plan to take $120 million dollars out of the company's $500 million annual operating budget. U.S. Surgical, which had never laid off a soul, now cut approximately 2,800 of its 8,500 global workforce. In addition, Hirsch put production workers on a four-day week, froze payrolls and slashed the dividend from $.30 to $.08 (which had a disproportionate impact on Hirsch, the largest U.S.S. stockholder). Finally, Leon Hirsch cut his own salary by 20 percent and those of his officers by 10 percent.

When asked if he was confident the rescue plan would work, Hirsch says emphatically, "No. I was scared to death. I didn't know if the cuts would be enough, given our falling sales. And we also had to raise money. Everything that could go wrong at that time went wrong. We had growth problems, quality problems, our marketplace was changing very fast and we had to deal with extremely tough competition from a huge company that was trying to bury us. I was worried, because the magnitude of our problems was greater than anything I'd ever faced. The first thing that I realized was that I couldn't fix U.S. Surgical by myself."

That recognition probably saved the company, and there was something heroically unsparing and unsentimental about it. This was his company, right down to the lab bench, where Hirsch, the inveterate tinkerer, would play with prototypes and make suggestions, like an auto executive bent on customizing his company's cars. But the prospect of losing everything he worked for, in Knarr's words, forced Hirsch to admit that he might also be wrong, and that he might need help. It must have been a painful admission, but the threat to U.S. Surgical's existence must have felt like near death.

"Early in 1993, on a Sunday, Hirsch called all the executives and a lot of the managers together, and he laid out the situation for us," says one executive. "There was no rancor, no shouting, just a statement of the situation as he saw it. He asked people for their personal commitment to fix things, and he told them he would give them the power to make the necessary changes in their own departments. Some of us took him at his word, and others decided that it was time to move on."

Hirsch, too, remembers that day. "I told everybody that we would have to come up with a new way of doing business that would reflect an entirely new set of realities. I also told them that the future of the company rested on their shoulders as much as mine. U.S. Surgical was going to have to become what we all made of it."

Rick Granger, vice president of research and development, was asked to reengineer his department to bring new products to market more rapidly; Josefsen was to restructure all international operations; Knarr's job was to develop a new strategy for selling; and accounting officer Howard Rosenkrantz was promoted to chief financial officer and given the tasks of convincing the banks to buy into the plan and turning U.S. Surgical into an efficient, rational, modern corporation. According to Knarr, "This was the first time that the company had ever really stepped away from the entrepreneurial style that it was famous for."

The executive group, given a clear mission, vigorously attacked the company's problems. The marketing department invited hundreds of operating room nurses, materials managers and administrators to its Norwalk, Connecticut, headquarters. They were called "VIP trips" and the customers were asked bluntly, Tell us what we're doing wrong. Out of such groups came a number of useful changes, including, for example, bundling U.S. Surgical products by procedure, so that everything the doctor needs to perform, say, a gallbladder operation, comes in a single package. That minimizes waste and saves money, as well as the potential for miscounted instruments, which might be lost in the patient and lead to a richly deserved malpractice suit.

Another part of the strategy was to find out exactly how U.S. Surgical was perceived within the hospital community. This was pretty easy: The company was seen as piratical and the salespeople as hustlers. In fact, surveys showed that the hospitals, the customers, barely tolerated U.S. Surgical people. Hirsch himself took on the grueling job of calling on dozens of hospital administrators, not to sell, but to listen to their complaints and promise improvements. Ultimately, the company determined that customer satisfaction was so important in the new managed care era that the entire compensation structure for the sales force was overhauled to reward it. This marked a complete reversal of Hirsch's traditional position that moving product and making every quarterly earnings estimate was paramount.

U.S.S. also began a Best Practices surgical management

program, which used proprietary cost and outcome data on common surgical procedures to help win back hospitals that had defected to Ethicon. Says Hirsch, "We told administrators that if they went with us, we would show them how to save thousands of dollars per procedure, far in excess of what our instruments cost. Instead of making the administrator an adversary, we made him a business partner."

Since putting the Best Practices program into operation, U.S. Surgical has recovered much of its business, and has scored some impressive wins over Johnson & Johnson, especially at prestigious teaching hospitals, such as Yale-New Haven, Emory University Medical Center (long an Ethicon customer), Baylor University Medical Center, Columbia Presbyterian, University of Pittsburgh Medical Center, Kaiser Permanente, and Cornell Medical centers.

Going still further, U.S.S. inaugurated what it calls Centers of Excellence, on-campus affiliations with eighteen of the country's leading teaching institutions, among them Harvard, Yale, Duke and Emory. The centers teach residents and practicing physicians laparoscopic surgery and are the sites of collaborative research projects between U.S.S. and the medical schools, aimed at developing new generations of surgical tools.

Within a year, U.S. Surgical had transformed itself. It was partnering with its customers, not sparring with them; it encouraged the best instincts of its salespeople through financial reward; it had broadened its decision-making ranks, strengthening its management capabilities; it was moving fast to expand its product base. With these changes in place, U.S. Surgical's sales and profits began to return to normal levels. The company earned $4.3 million on sales of $919 million in 1994. That year, Salomon Brothers, the big Wall Street bond trader, successfully sold $200 million in U.S. Surgical convertible bonds, ensuring that the company would have the cash it needed to rebuild. The numbers rose to $59.7 million and just above $1 billion, respectively, a year later. In 1996, sales rose again, above $1.1 billion, with net income rising to nearly $90 million.

All this began after Hirsch looked his business reality squarely in the face, shared what he saw with his colleagues, and asked them to join him in rebuilding the company. But the process of change, once begun, developed a logic and momentum of its own. U.S. Surgical jumped into the suture business, a business dominated by Johnson & Johnson. Says Hirsch, "We got into the suture business because we felt that to compete in the new economic world, bundling was very important. Every surgeon who uses a stapler also uses a suture, and many times in the same procedure. It turned out to be a very good move. The suture market is static, but we've been growing at an average of thirty percent a year for the last four years. Our suture business is well over a hundred-million-dollar business, which is about eight percent of the market."

Simultaneously, U.S. Surgical, with surprising nimbleness, began working toward becoming a broad-based medical technology enterprise. Once again, Hirsch saw he could not accomplish this single-handed, so a strategic planning staff was formed, as was a specialized group dedicated solely to canvassing the medical device and procedures market. Responsibility for day-to-day operations was given over to Rosenkrantz, now promoted to president and chief operating officer, and his senior executives, leaving Hirsch free to concentrate on growth opportunities.

Hirsch and U.S. Surgical signed more than a dozen agreements and made five acquisitions, spending over $600 million to support the goal of broadening their product offerings. Their first investment was a 9.5 percent equity stake in Alexion, a developer of transgenic products—including pig hearts, livers, lungs and kidneys—for human organ transplants. For its $4 million investment, plus up to another $7.5 million to support Alexion's research, U.S. Surgical picked up worldwide marketing rights to all of Alexion's products.

Over the next year and a half, the company licensed products from a number of cutting edge medical technology companies: a minimally invasive breast biopsy device; an advanced breast mammography system; a gynecological endoscope; a wound sealant that speeds healing. These deals were followed by the $60 million acquisition of Surgical Dynamics, Inc., whose spinal cage technology is key to the growing field of spinal surgery, with more than 200,000 procedures done worldwide each year. (SDI's sales jumped from $9 million to about $60 million in the next year alone.) And 1997 opened with a $75 million investment in Progressive Angioplasty Systems, which makes state-of-the-art coronary stents, the tubes that keep blocked arteries open and free of plaque after they are cleared—a global market in excess of $1 billion. Five months later, U.S.S. completed a deal for the rights to a technology that uses a tiny radioactive wire inside a blood vessel to prevent the plaque that causes the need for stents in the first place.

Perhaps U.S. Surgical's most vigorous initiative has been

in the field of cardiovascular surgery. Nearly three quarters of a million people a year undergo such operations annually, and the number is expected to grow as the population ages. They involve lots of trauma (cracking or sawing away ribs to get to the heart) and lots of money (total costs typically approach $100,000). In an effort to simplify these procedures, U.S. Surgical's research people have invented Mini-CABG, a set of tiny instruments that fit through a three-to-four-inch chest incision and allow a surgeon to work on a beating heart. This eliminates the heart-lung machine, and with it, a huge portion of the cost of open-heart surgery. Minimally invasive surgery is also far less traumatic to the patient, and requires a much shorter convalescence.

Ironically, says Granger, Mini-CABG was not one of those products that Hirsch was especially committed to. ABBI (U.S. Surgical's breast biopsy system) was another project that Hirsch didn't see much of a future in. That these projects went forward is in stark contrast to the old U.S. Surgical, Granger says, when research and investment initiatives generally came from Hirsch alone.

Ken Abramowitz, healthcare analyst for Sanford C. Bernstein & Son, agrees. The company now has a depth of management that it didn't have before. Other people besides Hirsch make decisions, and help sustain U.S. Surgical. For example, William Mavity, CEO of InnerDyne, which makes devices that control abnormal uterine bleeding, says he barely met Hirsch prior to entering into a joint marketing agreement. Other U.S.S. executives initiated the deal.

The company has also become a leader in a technique called transmyocardial revascularization, or TMR. TMR uses a tiny laser to shoot holes in the wall of the heart, creating passageways for blood to reach the wall of a failing heart, without damaging the heart muscle. In 1996, U.S. Surgical purchased Medolas GmbH, the number two company in TMR, and has been working to bring the technology through clinical trials. The procedure is working so well that it may become a preferred form of heart treatment within five years, supplementing bypass surgery to bring more blood to the heart.

All these deals were a prelude to U.S. Surgical's December 1997 acquisition, for $425 million, of the Valleylab division of Pfizer, Inc., with its leading edge electrosurgical and ultrasonic products. Valleylab will add an immediate $200 million in sales annually to U.S. Surgical's top line.

Why take on so many different, and sometimes competing, technologies? U.S. Surgical executives note that, while the range may be broad, all still revolve around calling on surgeons, speaking their language and helping find better ways for them to do their work in the operating room. "The skills are the same," says Knarr. "Identify areas where we can bring either technology or marketing expertise to a deal with a potential partner, or both. And we report to each other what the doctors and hospitals are saying about a particular technology or procedure. Then we go out and see if we can get an agreement."

This way of proceeding, which strongly emphasizes initiative and collaboration, has given the whole company a new image of itself and its goal. "Today," says Hirsch, "our culture is innovation. We're not in wound closure or suturing, we're innovators. Once we decided that the entire field of surgery was open to us, the possibilities became much greater than they ever were before. We're looking into areas we would never have dreamed of before our business got into trouble. And it's rounding the company out so that we have much less exposure to a single competitor in a single market."

Hirsch's goal was for his new products and acquisitions to bring U.S. Surgical's sales to $2 billion by the year 2000 and double earnings as well. It's an aggressive plan and so far, says Abramowitz of Sanford C. Bernstein & Son, the jury is out. "But the company took the breast biopsy business from nothing to fifty million dollars in sales in just two years, and they took the orthopedic business [SDI] from nothing to more than one hundred million dollars in the same period of time. That's fifteen percent growth for a one-billion-dollar company. If they have five other successful diversification moves like that, this will be a very strong company."

In the meantime, the changes in the culture and mission of U.S. Surgical have begun to change the way the company is seen in the marketplace. Says Mavity, "When we first decided to do a deal with U.S. Surgical, about four different people called me up and suggested that I was crazy, given their reputation, to get in bed with them. But we talked to a number of other companies, and when we had to choose, we chose them because they do things in a timely manner, they are thoroughly professional and they do what they promise. I only know the old U.S. Surgical by reputation. And that reputation is not the company I have been dealing with."

For his part, Hirsch emphatically says, "Is this a different company? Of course it is. The times are different, and U.S.

Surgical requires a different set of skills to run it. When I started, I was working in my basement. Now we're heading for two billion dollars in sales. I can't do everything, but I don't have to. I'm surrounded by talented people."

Possibly the ultimate measure of how much Hirsch has changed comes from the fact that *he* proposed to his friend Tyco chairman Dennis Koslowski that their companies join forces. Koslowski was delighted with the idea, saying he would meet to talk to Hirsch about it at 6 A.M. the next morning, if he wished. But he had never dreamed of making such a proposal to Hirsch, for fear of insulting him. No one, probably, imagined Hirsch would ever consent to any agreement that might reduce his independence. And in fact, just prior to the Tyco deal, he and his board had rejected an unsolicited merger proposal.

Prior to the merger with Tyco, the one place where Hirsch's new direction hadn't played well was on Wall Street. Despite recent quarters that brought the strongest sales and profit growth since 1992, Wall Street took a wait-and-see attitude, based on the looming presence of Ethicon in U.S. Surgical's key markets and the continuing uncertainty about healthcare payments. The stock, as of mid-1998, was trading in the low-to-mid 30s, well off its 1994 floor, but far from its pre-endoscopic heights. Still, out of nearly twenty analysts who regularly followed the company, only a few like John Runningen, an analyst with Robinson-Humphrey in Atlanta, were decisively upbeat.

More typical was Abramowitz, who cautioned, "He's built a strong management team, but entrepreneurs think they're going to live forever. Until he totally empowers the management by naming his successor, there will always be some reservations about the future of U.S. Surgical."

Now, all that has changed. The Tyco merger will create a $4.5 billion medical products powerhouse, which [Tyco Chairman] Dennis Koslowski has asked Hirsch to run (he will also become Tyco's first inside director). The prospect of competing on an equal footing with the other medical products giants is clearly one Hirsch relishes. He says, smiling, "I think we can develop a business plan that will integrate perhaps twenty to twenty-five product lines, and be able to present to a hospital fifty percent of their operating needs from one source. We will be the clear-cut number two medical device company in the world—J&J being number one—and we're after making ourselves number one. That's the challenge I have now."

Hirsch jokes that his new job will "never distance me from U.S. Surgical because their offices will still be up the hall." It's also possible that Hirsch, into his seventh decade, finally accepts that his corporate child will go on without him one day. At some point during the company's crisis, Hirsch says, "I realized that I had created an institution with a life of its own. It has to be able to function, to be competitive, to excel in the marketplace whether I'm here or not."

Still, when asked whether age and past accomplishments have produced a satisfied, less driven Leon Hirsch, he just laughs. Then he adds, "I intend to be around for a long time to come."

8/Robert Louis-Dreyfus
Don't Worry, Be Happy

On September 15, 1997, Adidas AG chairman Robert Louis-Dreyfus raised a fluted glass at the elegant Hôtel des Bergues in Geneva, Switzerland, to toast his company's acquisition of Salomon S.A., the high-tech, highly profitable French athletic equipment maker. It was not a ceremonial toast; the fifty-one-year-old Louis-Dreyfus adores good food and wine, and would never willingly forgo a glass of good champagne.

There were many reasons to celebrate. The Salomon family was beaming at the $1.4 billion price tag. And Adidas investors also had reason to cheer, since Salomon's high-margin skiing, golfing and biking products would diversify the Adidas portfolio, reducing its dependence on low-margin, marketing intensive items like sneakers and T-shirts. Industry analysts also noted Adidas would be able to pay for the whole thing out of earnings.

But it was Louis-Dreyfus to whom the day belonged, capping four remarkable years as head of Adidas. Having rescued one of Europe's best-known brands from near death, he had now transformed it into the world's second-biggest sports equipment firm, one well positioned to take on the still larger Nike Corp. in an expected war for supremacy in a $100 billion market. His career, *The Economist* magazine averred, could now be seen as a "parable" for how modern, efficient and competitive the best business minds on the continent could be.

This recognition may have been the sweetest accomplishment of all. Louis-Dreyfus has a famous name (he was born in the same village as his ancestor Captain Dreyfus; *Seinfeld* actress Julia Louis-Dreyfus is a relative) and his family is among the wealthiest in France, with assets in the billions of dollars. Louis Dreyfus & Cie was founded in 1851 by his great-great-great-grandfather, and today, according to *Forbes* magazine, trades $22 billion annually in commodities, owns huge amounts of office space, has its own cargo fleet and is the world's third-largest orange juice producer, among numerous other ventures. And it remains a family firm, one for which Robert Louis-Dreyfus worked for seven years. Then, in 1981, he left. "When there are too many in a family business, it's difficult," he says today. "There were too many brothers, sisters, uncles, cousins and so on. I knew I would never have a chance to run it, so better to leave and not be frustrated twenty years later."

He had made a lot of money in his previous ventures. Now, not quite twenty years later, he had made his mark.

◼

In April 1993, a consortium of desperate European lenders, led by Credit Lyonnais, France's largest bank, virtually gave away control of Adidas to Dreyfus and his partner Christian Tourres.

For $10,000 each, the price of a compact car, the two men and a small group of friends bought 15 percent of the venerable German athletic shoe and apparel firm. In addition, they were granted the right to purchase the remaining 85 percent at a fixed price after eighteen months, and given a $100 million nonrecourse loan (so-called because the lenders had "no recourse" if the borrowers couldn't pay it back).

The catch? Adidas was a dead horse in an industry at full gallop. Company founder Adi Dassler had died in 1978, followed by his son Horst in 1987. They were succeeded by a series of inept leaders, either "managers," as they are scornfully referred to around company headquarters, or worse. The last was a flamboyant French politician named Bernard Tapie, who bought the company in 1990 for around $300 million. But the money was borrowed, Tapie couldn't service the debt and was, in any case, soon on his way to jail for fixing a soccer game, among other things.

By the time the banks took control in 1992, Adidas had degenerated into a jumble of brand names—Le Coq Sportif, Pony, Adidas—which, says one Adidas executive, made or licensed the right to make, "coats, ties, perfume, everything." The core shoe division, meanwhile, had developed a tragicomic reputation for producing dubious products, like expensive jogging shoes with built-in computers that broke when customers laced them up. It was, says creative director Peter Moore, "A company that had lost its soul, that really didn't know what it was supposed to be doing."

Adidas lost tens of millions of dollars annually starting in the late 1980s, culminating in a $100 million loss in 1992. Sales in that year were about $1.5 billion, half a billion dollars *less* than a decade before. The majority of those losses stemmed from the United States, where Adidas's share of the running shoe market had shrunk to a microscopic 1.9 percent in 1992, from an astonishing 70 percent two decades earlier. At one particularly depressing moment in the late 1980s, Adidas's sole hot-selling item was a line of Olympic Games sweatshirts.

Given this background, it is perhaps not surprising that the company came within one meeting of closing its doors in October 1992. In fact, Adidas survived only because a former German finance minister, who served on the company's supervisory board, assembled some thirty creditors in Munich and convinced them not to cut off financing.

Still, the banks, having foreclosed on Tapie, were left with a property nobody wanted at any price. Nike itself, one of its executives later told Louis-Dreyfus, had been offered Adidas for less money than Tourres and Louis-Dreyfus would ultimately pay for it. "[Nike Chairman] Phil Knight asked whether Reebok would buy the company if Nike didn't," Dreyfus says. "When his aides said no, he supposedly said, 'Well, then, they'll die by their own hand.' "

It must have been a nice moment for Knight, the rabidly

competitive former middle-distance runner who reportedly had once vowed to "tear down Adidas, down to the last pair of running shoes in Berlin."

The unlikely setting for this corporate drama was Herzogenaurach ("Herzo" in local parlance), a medieval Franconian village of ten thousand or so souls, where shoemaking had been the dominant trade for generations.

Just after World War I, a baker (albeit a cobbler's son) named Adolf "Adi" Dassler began making bedroom slippers out of discarded U.S. Army tires and tent canvas. Adi loved sports, however, and soon switched to manufacturing running and soccer shoes. So fixated was he on improving athletes' performance through better shoes that he attached the factory to the back of his house, the better to tinker at all hours. (In an odd historical parallel, Nike, too, began with a pedomane. Bill Bowerman, Phil Knight's track coach at Oregon University and later his business partner and shoe guru, spent so much time gluing together experimental shoe materials in his unventilated basement workshop that he developed a fatal neuromuscular illness from breathing toxic fumes.)

Sales grew steadily and Adi's shoes developed a pan-European clientele. They found their way into the 1928 Amsterdam Olympics, and four years later, in Los Angeles, several athletes won medals in them. Then, in 1936, the Dassler *Schuhfabriken* produced the shoes Jesse Owens used to win four gold medals at the Berlin Olympics. Instantly, Owens became the most celebrated athlete of his time, while Dassler appeared poised for commercial stardom as an equipment maker. World War II, however, intervened. Adi joined the Nazi Party and retooled to produce boots for the Wehrmacht.

The *Schuhfabriken* survived the war unscathed, as did Herzogenaurach, but in 1948 Adi and his brother Rudi split after a bitter quarrel (local legend has it that Rudi couldn't figure out why he had to go fight while Adi got to stay home and make shoes). Adi renamed his company Adidas, while Rudi immediately started the rival Puma shoe company on the other side of the village.

A few years later, in 1954, Adi's shoes with replaceable cleats helped the German soccer team win the World Cup on a muddy field. The victory provoked a huge celebration and Adi became a celebrity in a nation eager to supplant recent memories with new heroes. Daily shoe production jumped from eight hundred to two thousand pairs, as the sports world descended on this figure out of Grimm, who made champions from his bench in a rural village guarded by ruined twelfth-century watchtowers.

By the 1960s, Adi and Käthe, his marketing-savvy wife, were the most powerful figures in international athletics. During the 1972 Munich Olympics (the year Nike was incorporated) more than 80 percent of the gold medalists wore Adidas shoes and every Olympic official wore Adidas-designed uniforms. By mid-decade, three-quarters of NBA basketball players wore the three stripes, as did every soccer team worth its shorts. When Adi Dassler died at age seventy-seven, his brand was recognized by an estimated 95 percent of the world.

At the time of Adi's death, the company had literally grown up around him. You can still see the Dassler house, a modest, two-story stucco dwelling known locally as "the Villa," nearly engulfed by the jumble of buildings and walkways that make up the compact Adidas headquarters.

In fact, the physical layout became a metaphor for the company's problems. After so many years of family control and a virtual monopoly on competition-quality shoes and clothes, Adidas had totally lost touch with the marketplace. It was, says Jan Valdmaa, the young Swedish executive vice president and director of global marketing, "an isolated manufacturing company with a distribution strategy." That strategy, incidentally, was utterly mad.

Buyers and distributors would arrive in Herzogenaurach, stay at the hotel Adi and Käthe had built for them, and review the products Adidas had decided to manufacture. Then they would head for Alsace where, in a family apparently fated to internecine conflict, Horst Dassler, after a quarrel with his sisters, had created a mirror-image Adidas, with its own factories and products. Incredibly, buyers would "go price shopping" (in the words of a senior executive who witnessed the process), pitting the two Adidases against each other to bargain for better prices.

Michel Perraudin, an executive vice president, remembers coming to Herzo in 1987 as part of a McKinsey & Co. consulting team that had been called in to tell Adidas's management what was going wrong. Back then, he says,

Adidas senior managers still felt, "We are the holder of the Biblical truths as far as a pair of sneakers is concerned. This is the sneaker and the sneaker is good."

The cost of this arrogant provincialism ultimately amounted to billions. For example, it surely led the company to spurn Frank Ruby, an inventor who in the 1970s offered it the rights to the indestructible little air bags that are the heart of Nike's "Air" technology. And when Michael Jordan left college for the NBA in 1984, he *wanted* to endorse Adidas, not Nike. Adidas had always been his favorite shoe, and he asked only for a deal comparable to the $3 million over five years, plus his own shoe model, that Nike was offering. The wizards of Franconia couldn't be bothered.

Another problem was that Adidas manufactured its own shoes at its own European factories. In 1987, the company employed roughly fifteen thousand people, most in factory jobs at generous European wage-and-benefit levels. But Nike, Reebok and everyone else simply outsourced production to wherever the labor was cheap and the quality could be assured. This meant they could keep prices down *and* maintain profit margins, while Adidas faced the Hobson's choice of pricing their shoes competitively, but losing money, or raising prices above their rivals and losing sales. Either way, Adidas had ever less cash to spend, to the point that it could no longer buy airtime for the few commercials it could afford to shoot of its small stable of star endorsers, such as Steffi Graf. As Peter Moore recalls, "There were some pretty bad times here. There were literally days when you didn't know if this was the last day the company was going to be in business."

Access to senior executives on the "fifth floor," a circle of office suites on the top floor of the tallest Adidas building, was strictly guarded. Mid-level employees who wanted to meet with fifth-floor denizens were required to write detailed meeting agenda memos, which were returned for *revision* before an audience would be granted or denied. Absurdly, in a village with no crime to speak of, fifth-floor executives closeted themselves behind a locked security door under electronic surveillance, with a security guard stationed to scrutinize and buzz in visitors. Louis-Dreyfus's predecessor, Rene Jäggi, required personal bodyguards. As Herbert Hainer, director of European sales, recalls, Adidas "was like a bank—everybody wearing blue suits and ties. And we were acting like a bank, not a sports marketing company."

These antique rituals were preserved even as sports and the sports shoe industry were metamorphosing into show business. It was, as Perraudin says, "an industry on fire, with major new competitors which, right from the beginning, were market driven and consumer driven. Our competitors' point of view was, 'What does the consumer want? He wants soft, pink leather? Fine.' "

The industry was not only growing spectacularly in commercial terms, but in cultural influence, as well. Amid the wild proliferation of ads, logos and slogans, one writer for an American news magazine half-jokingly wrote that the military-industrial complex had been supplanted by a "media-sneaker complex" that had infiltrated our dreams and desires. Shoemakers were expected to respond to every trend, every whim or fantasy of the consumer. But Adidas stayed rooted in deeply conservative Franconia, where, says Peter Csanadi, the Hungarian-born director of public relations, "you will always get exactly the same size schnitzel and dumpling in every village restaurant." The fifth floor couldn't even begin to understand the changes sweeping through their business.

"Adidas certainly pioneered the development of athletic footwear," said Nike designer Tinker Hatfield, in *Just Do It,* Donald Katz's book about Nike's corporate culture. But, he said, "They still don't understand how to go beyond that and design in romance and imagery and all of those subliminal characteristics that make an object important to people in less utilitarian ways."

One of the most telling aspects—never reported in the press—of Louis-Dreyfus's royal progress at Adidas is that the banks initially turned to Christian Tourres to save their investment. It was Tourres, Louis-Dreyfus's friend and longtime colleague at IMS International, a medical marketing firm, who insisted that Louis-Dreyfus be given the job.

London-based IMS was run by David Dubow, an American who, starting in the early 1960s, built the company from five people—among them Tourres—to several thousand. Dubow was committed to creating a collaborative culture, many years before words like collaboration or culture figured in the vocabulary of every executive. "Dubow taught all of us, including Robert, the basics of teamwork and showed us that it works," said Tourres. "This is one of the keys to our success at Adidas." This culture held firm even after Dubow named Louis-Dreyfus his successor, to the initial disappointment of several executives of much longer tenure, including Tourres.

Louis-Dreyfus had joined IMS in 1981 as chief operating officer. One story, perhaps apocryphal, but in keeping with Louis-Dreyfus's self-presentation, has it that he met Dubow at an IMS board meeting, where he was a stand-in for a friend to whom he owed a poker debt. In any case, two years later Louis-Dreyfus was named CEO, at which time, the company had a market capitalization of $400 million. Louis-Dreyfus kept the company tightly focused on its niche, pulling it back from several ventures outside the medical market, and IMS grew rapidly over the next five years, when it was sold to Dun & Bradstreet for $1.7 billion. Top officers walked away with about $10 million each.

At this point Tourres and Louis-Dreyfus, eight years his junior, decided to retire to a life of directorships and leisurely investing. "Robert and I had a few businesses here and there—investments only—and I was in touch with a number of the banks dealing with them." Tourres recalls. "One of them, Banque de Phénix, called me and asked, 'Are you interested in running Adidas?' I said no. They called me back three or four times, until I got fed up and said, even if I was [interested] I would only do it with my partner, and the banker said, fine. So I called Robert."

But in 1991 Louis-Dreyfus was a headhunter's nightmare. Back in 1988, against the advice of his friends, he had accepted the entreaties of the Saatchi brothers to salvage the giant Saatchi & Saatchi advertising agency in London. At the time, it was a huge, swaying, house of cards, assembled through debt-backed acquisition, and Louis-Dreyfus spent much of the next three years simply buying time to cut costs. This meant repeatedly going hat in hand to the banks for money, and begging, says his friend Tourres, "is not the style of the Louis-Dreyfus family, especially with banks."

Every cash infusion gave Louis-Dreyfus breathing room to divest a few assets, shed some jobs and slash some expenses. It was grueling, thankless triage, laying the groundwork for Saatchi & Saatchi's ultimate recovery, but not taking the company in any new direction. It was hardly the sort of work for a man who didn't have to work. No wonder Louis-Dreyfus initially told Tourres that the last thing in the world he wanted was another turnaround. Eventually, however, as Adidas's hapless creditors kept sweetening the deal, the two would-be retirees caved in. "For the fun of it," they both said. But Louis-Dreyfus insisted before signing the contract that the banks loan the company $100 million up front—no more begging. With no other hope of saving their investment, the banks agreed.

Why did Tourres insist that Louis-Dreyfus occupy the CEO's chair? The question has several answers. Tourres said, "It would be much more fun to do this with him than without him," and, under the circumstances, it's hard not to believe him. The two men are good friends and partners of long standing, with obvious respect and affection for each other. Tourres lives comfortably and privately, and he loathes the ceremonial elements of executive position—the endless public relations events, investor meetings, magazine and newspaper interviews—that are critical to a sports company, which sells image as much as substance. Louis-Dreyfus, on the other hand, loves the company of athletes and seems to enjoy the celebrity and hoopla of big-time sports. Then, too, there are the lessons inculcated by David Dubow. As Tourres puts it, "I am a great believer that two heads are better than one. It worked very, very well at IMS."

Beyond that, Louis-Dreyfus seems to inspire a remarkable degree of faith and affection, in Tourres and in everyone else. Even at Saatchi, where many people were fired and many subsidiaries were sold, he remained well liked and respected. Indeed, long before Robert arrived in Herzo, Saatchi's London secretaries had told their counterparts in Herzo that Louis-Dreyfus was "special." That he was approachable, straightforward and unusually considerate.

Finally, Tourres says, adding a nice touch of *realpolitik*, "Robert is damn smart and he has a name, on top of his own strengths and intelligence. The fact that he is called Louis-Dreyfus helps a lot, he knows a lot of financial people—he has introductions everywhere."

Louis-Dreyfus and Tourres arrived in April 1993. Tourres looks more or less like a lot of French executives; he's trim, impeccably groomed and turned out, but in nicely tailored sports coats and loafers, not three-piece suits. Louis-Dreyfus, on the other hand, is habitually referred to in the press as "rumpled." In fact, he can look like an unmade bed. He's a tall man, a bit pear-shaped, with unruly curly hair and a mobile, slightly jowly face that is irregularly shaven and regularly creased by laughter. A sartorial eccentric, he's generally outfitted in old polo shirts, blue jeans, sneakers (or, in the office, barefoot), and often has a large Havana cigar in his mouth. The overall impression is of relaxed informality and self-confidence. Only the eyes belie this effect. They are alert, intelligent and not infrequently something like suspicion or impatience troubles their surface.

It's hard to overstress the effect Louis-Dreyfus's appearance and manner had at Adidas. Tourres laughingly says that the Germans are "a serious people, but they need a little bit of a Latin atmosphere." They got it. "When Robert came," says Tom Harrington, the director of communications, "you could almost feel the difference right away. He came in and walked around in his bare feet. Nobody knew what to make of him. I'm sure the Germans didn't."

Herbert Hainer, himself German and a recruit from the soldierly ranks of Procter & Gamble to boot, recalls, "When Robert joined, everybody knew this is Robert Louis-Dreyfus, the son or the brother or the something of the rich Dreyfus family. But then Robert came in with his jeans and his polo shirt; he was like everybody else. In a room of two hundred Adidas people, you couldn't tell who was Mr. Robert Louis-Dreyfus. It gave the people, without saying much, the feeling that 'I'm like you, we are a team.' "

The next thing everyone noticed was that, in a company that had been rife with internal politics, Robert and Christian were harmoniously collaborative, invariably civil. There was a good-humored Alphonse and Gaston sort of affection between the two men—please, you first, oh no, I couldn't, you first—that was reflected not only in Tourres's ceding power to Louis-Dreyfus, but in his often throwing it back to Tourres. "Robert and Christian" became a kind of mantra, a synecdochical phrase that signified a way of operating.

More than that, these two men were winners, coming to a team that had been on a long losing streak, and their self-confidence was sorely needed. As Perraudin says, "I think it has been inherent to the success of the organization that at no point in time did either Robert or Christian give the feeling—or have the feeling—that they could fail. I think for them it was sort of a done deal all along."

It was a confidence born of experience, not braggadocio. Mary Friday, the Adidas general counsel who worked with both men at IMS, says, "These men are incredibly energetic; they bring a sense of vitality and life to a problem. They are very clear thinkers, so they make decisions, and they instill in people a sense that failure is not something to be afraid of." And of Robert in particular, she notes, "One thing you don't see is how well trained he is; there's nothing lacking; he absorbs information, discerns key issues, has a clear sense of direction and delegates comfortably."

It was, it must be said, an opportune moment for new leadership. Previous regimes at Adidas had done two things right since 1987, when Horst Dassler died. First, following the McKinsey analysis, they had drastically reduced manufacturing capacity, cutting the head count from 15,000 to about 5,500. Robert swiftly shed the remaining French and German plants. Second, Rob Strasser and his partner Peter Moore, the duo who saved Nike by creating and marketing the Air Jordan line, had formed a sports marketing operation. Retained as consultants in 1989, they urged Adidas to shed peripheral products and activities, and go back to its roots in high performance athletic shoes and clothes. Strasser also suggested a new business structure, one divided not by functions, such as marketing, accounting or manufacturing, but by sports. Each "Business Unit Structure" and its manager, or BUM, would concentrate on one sport—soccer, tennis, or track and field—overseeing every aspect of design, marketing, production schedules, budgets and so on.

Strasser, who told the press that Adidas "had taken nine bullets to the head" and survived, combed the company for "young, dumb and cheap" people who loved sports and could help him to revive the brand. When he set up the BUM system in 1991, Tom Harrington recalls, "He tried to find the best guys around the company, and those are the guys who built the foundation of the success we have today by starting to make better products. When times got bad, those guys on the fifth floor sat up in their offices and closed their doors. The turnaround at Adidas was not accomplished by 'management'; it was begun by a bunch of guys who believed in the brand, believed in the company and who cared."

Jan Valdmaa, then in his mid-thirties, was brought from Stockholm to Herzo. He recalls that Strasser's Young Turks set up a series of small units, with no formal power, each dedicated to producing and marketing Moore's back-to-basics line of gear called "Adidas Equipment." "We were like islands in this place," Valdmaa recalls. "We had almost no contact with the rest of the organization. And then the older part of the organization just sort of evaporated, and suddenly we were able to do more and more."

Within weeks of his arrival Louis-Dreyfus dismissed the entire German senior management, with the exception of Perraudin. This was not an arbitrary act, he says today. "I said, we have to transform this from a manufacturing company to a marketing company and we needed some outside people. It was a very inbred culture. How can you run a multinational company if you've never traveled beyond Nuremberg? You had to bring in some new blood."

Next came a quick trip to Asia, where a small and ineffective sourcing operation had been set up to oversee manufacturing. That crew, too, was fired, and a new sourcing director, Glenn Bennett, was hired away from Reebok to build a professional pan-Asian operation. Today, Adidas has six hundred people engaged in the complex and critical enterprise of getting their products made as well and cheaply as possible, whether in Vietnam or China or Thailand. And the company has thus far avoided the charges of using exploited labor that have recently plagued Nike.

On his return to Herzo Louis-Dreyfus threw out all the fifth-floor security apparatus and was soon seen daily—bodyguardless—on the jogging paths of Herzo. He moved his own office into another building, smack in the middle of the marketing group. Jan Valdmaa, who was startled at the time to find himself working cheek by jowl with the CEO, says, "The way Robert came in was very much as part of the brand. He had direct contact with product managers; there was a lack of hierarchy. The organization became very flat. We had him beside us and everyone with an idea could act on it, which sorted out the politics in the company.

"It was always very easy to see him; you came up with the thing you wanted to do and he said, 'Okay' if he didn't have a problem with it. There was no discussion, to the point where you almost wanted to ask him, 'Don't you want me to submit a plan before I do this?' This should be a pretty difficult company to run, but it doesn't look that way when you're around him. He deals with things very easily."

Robert had seen that Adidas, whatever its other problems, was starving the brand. As its competitors poured money into every conceivable marketing niche, Adidas had faded to near invisibility. Louis-Dreyfus responded by using a good chunk of the $100 million he had demanded from the banks to immediately double the marketing budget. Then, in a gesture of enormous symbolic significance, he conducted an advertising agency review. Everyone at Adidas assumed that the account would be taken from the incumbent agency, Leagus Delaney, and given to Saatchi & Saatchi. Not only did Dreyfus have friends there, Saatchi had made an investment in Adidas. Harrington remembers, "[Robert] came from Saatchi; Saatchi was a part owner. So it was quite obvious that Saatchi was going to become our agency. Then they came in and made a great flashy presentation, but they didn't understand sport, they didn't understand our business, the ideas were terrible. They just didn't get it."

Bob McCullough, then Harrington's boss, and Harrington decided to tell Robert not to change agencies. "We gave him the reasons," Harrington said. "It was a pretty tough indictment, because this was the agency he had just run. He could have fired us, but he basically said, if that's your recommendation, you're the guys who have to live with the consequences. You have to respect a guy who demands from you your honest opinion and who will support it. His ego didn't get in the way."

In addition, Tourres and Louis-Dreyfus made it a priority to hire young people from all over the world to break up the old culture. Today there are employees from twenty-two different countries at the Herzo headquarters, and the official language of the company is English. Louis-Dreyfus also established Nike's hometown of Beaverton, Oregon, as the headquarters for his U.S. operation.

Finally, at a company full of sports-loving ex-jocks, Louis-Dreyfus proved to be a genuine sports fanatic and a marathon runner, for whom athletes were heroes. He knew more about current soccer players' statistics than the Adidas promotions director, and Peter Csanadi says that the company has even shifted the starting time of the annual shareholders meeting so that Louis-Dreyfus could make it to the finals of a European soccer championship.

Like most athletes, Louis-Dreyfus is also intensely competitive. Mostly, this desire to win is hidden behind an ursine friendliness, but it can flash forth in startling fashion. Once, for example, Louis-Dreyfus was pulling into the Adidas parking lot when a messenger making a delivery crossed in front of his car. Like messengers around the world, he was wearing sneakers, but they weren't Adidas, and Louis-Dreyfus erupted. "What's that goddamned asshole wearing on his feet!" he shouted. He wants to win every match, precisely the right attitude at a company where, as one manager puts it, "You've got to know the smell of the locker room, to know about sport, to work here."

■

So, Adidas was ready. It had transformed its manufacturing model, it had a core group of bright, committed young executives, and, for the first time in a long time, it had capital. Harrington, who joined Adidas in 1988 and calls himself, "the rat who climbed onto the sinking ship," says the foundation existed for a renaissance. "But we needed leadership," he says, "someone to tell us we were on the right course, doing the right things."

In the event, the turnaround came so fast that even Robert and Christian were surprised. In their first year, 1993, the fashion world decided that the old Adidas three-stripe logo, was "retro," and hence cool. Madonna was seen wearing Adidas, so were the rappers Run DMC and models Claudia Schiffer and Cindy Crawford. This fortuitous stylishness helped jump-start the company's new products and marketing efforts, and Adidas closed out the year with a $4.7 million profit, after the previous year's $100 million loss. Peter Csanadi wanted to trumpet this "tremendous turnaround" in the annual report, but Robert told him, "Nine million [expletive] Deutsche marks—I'm not so proud of this that I want to tell everyone how wise I am."

The next year, though, the company earned about $100 million. The sales organization blunted and began to roll back Nike's European charge, and Christian also began to buy back, either wholly or by way of a majority stake, the various independent national subsidiaries, giving Adidas control of how its products were marketed and sold. This time Robert did tell the press, "The Adidas renaissance is now proven. For the first time in many years, revenues will stop declining." And at the company's Christmas party, he announced, to a cheering crowd, that every worker should henceforth share in Adidas's success, starting with an extra month's salary.

The recovery took a quantum leap in 1995, with year-end profits of $163 million on sales of $3.4 billion. Moreover, Louis-Dreyfus and Tourres pulled off a spectacularly successful initial public offering of its shares, or IPO, late in the year, raising about $2 billion. (The shares were priced at $42.50 and, as of March 1998, were up more than 400 percent). A year later, profits rose to $209 million, and demand for a new, technologically advanced line of footwear, "Feet You Wear," outstripped supply.

Nineteen ninety-seven brought only more good news. Net income rose 48 percent, to $255 million, and sales rose 23 percent. U.S. sales, climbing at a blistering 50 percent a year, will be about $1.5 billion in 1998, by which time Adidas will have captured more than 7 percent of the market (up from 1.9 percent in 1992). Meanwhile, Adidas has "become almost as trendy as Nike," according to *The Economist*. U.S. investors will soon get their shot at the company, with Adidas American Depositary Receipts (ADRs) soon to be available here. "In the next few years," says Louis-Dreyfus, "we're going to grow to ten to fifteen percent of [the] U.S. market, which is aggressive. I'm ready to spend over the next four to five years fifteen to seventeen percent of [our] budget on marketing. We're already a billion-dollar company in the States, so we're talking about $170 million. At that level, you start to be a presence. Other than Nike and Reebok, nobody else will have the same marketing power."

Meanwhile, the newly cash-rich Adidas will begin to use its marketing muscle to go head-to-head with Nike for shelf space, athlete endorsements and advertising visibility. And the Salomon acquisition will give him instant access to golf pro shops and ski shops, a whole new distribution channel. Moreover, Salomon makes no apparel, creating an opportunity for Adidas to create whole new lines, especially for skiing and Salomon's Taylor Made premium brand of golf equipment.

The question, of course, is, what happened? Christian downplays the "heroic" leadership angle, saying, "We did nothing dramatic, really. That is the funny thing. The company had a tremendous brand name, but it needed just common sense to restore it. It was really only a matter of restoring confidence inside the company. Give a goal, give a target to people. Some people will talk to you for hours about how good they have been, but I think anyone could have done it, with a little normal common sense."

When pressed, he will reluctantly allow that he and Robert were at least good cheerleaders. "It's a little embarrassing, things like this, but I think they [the employees] feel that the company has a goal, know where it's going, what its objectives are, when in the past only a very small number of people at the top had an opinion where they wanted the company to go, but didn't share it. And that makes a difference.

"Also, I would say that not having problems at the top, with the two of us, helped a lot with the young people who wanted to make a career here by killing their rivals. We said, look, take us as an example, you don't need to kill your neighbor to succeed. There's room enough for everyone in the company to succeed.

"We are basically both of us extremely lazy, which

means the less we work the better it is. We have told all the guys, you want to grow up, and the company needs you to grow up because one day we will have to leave. So you do the job and if the results are there, we won't interfere. I think this message has come through very clear and it is why we now have an excellent team coming up."

Robert, too, is invincibly urbane and ironic about leadership (he told *Time* magazine a couple of years ago that he knew nothing about the sneaker business and was only copying Nike and Reebok). On first broaching the subject, he says, "With hindsight, in most of my business career, I find that people, if you go to them and say, 'Look, here's my plan, I have every reason to believe it will work, but you know I could be wrong,' they will show themselves to be much more responsible than you think.

"At Adidas I think I convinced people to follow me by default, because they had such a lack of leadership since Horst Dassler died in 1987. I was pretty upfront in saying, here are the people we need to get rid of, here is where I think things are not working, et cetera. Once it was on the table—no uncertainty.

"I treat people the same way, which, especially for a German company, is unusual. And I frown upon senior people who don't do that. I don't send them a memo, but I try to joke with them about it. I try to have a sense of humor, and if you let them laugh at you then half of the battle is won."

When Louis-Dreyfus tosses off such bromides, it's easy to miss the breadth of business experience that underlies them. After he got his MBA from Harvard, for example, he returned to Paris to join the family. "My family couldn't care less if I had an MBA or not," he says. "So they sent me to work in a factory in Brazil, as number four, at a crushing plant, in a little town that makes Herzo look like the capital of the world. It deflates your ego. You learn very quickly if you are on the ground (and I didn't speak Portuguese well) that practical things, contact with people works."

When asked whether leadership can be taught, he replies, "No. I think that's rubbish. They [MBA programs] may give you things to think about. They may give you a breviary, like a bible. I'm the worst speaker in the world; I can't make a rousing speech; if I analyze myself, I don't think I have many qualities of what the business school would think of as leadership. I don't project self-assuredness, motivation, et cetera.

"I think I'm a great motivator one-on-one—sorry, a good motivator. Making a compliment to myself, I listen to people. Also, I always tell them, you can make mistakes; that's the way you learn. The only thing is always come back to me when you've made a mistake. We can try to sort it out. But don't give me a bad surprise when it's too late to do something. The only way you learn is by tripping.

"That's why we encourage disagreement, to get people to open up. One reason we got rid of existing management was that they liked to hear what they wanted to hear. People are pretty frank with me. They are not, really not, afraid of me. There has to be irreverence, so that not only is someone allowed to tell me I'm wrong, but there's a culture where it's better to say we disagree than we agree. In the end they have to have the respect, hopefully, that when you say, okay, I've heard all of you and I think we have to do this, that nobody will second-guess. That's leadership."

9/CONCLUSION
The Reality Principle

The British management theoretician Charles Handy calls this the Age of Uncertainty, an epoch of incessant, extreme and often unforseeable shifts in business conditions—"discontinuous change," in Handy's words. No wonder the abstruse realm of "chaos" theory has been adopted by executives to describe the view from their office windows.

It's the sort of world in which the Encyclopedia Brittanica company, accustomed for over a century to charging a premium price for a superb product, suddenly found that it had to abandon its massive volumes for a single disc of plastic called a CD-ROM. Then the company, suffering from plummeting sales and falling profits, discovered no one would pay the thousand or so dollars the business plan called for. Today, restructured and under new ownership, the company is trying again, this time at $125 for each disc.

All of us are still struggling to understand this brave new world. We level organizational pyramids to create "flat," agile organizations that continually "learn," while we attempt to keep our best "symbolic analysts" sufficiently motivated and compensated to stay and work at peak performance. Leadership is seen as the indispensable motor, the prime mover, behind this activity, and yet we still understand little about what makes a good leader and even less how to produce one. Here, for example, is a passage from a distinguished professor of management on how leaders communicate:

"The simplest explanation of how leaders get their message across is through charisma in that one of the main elements of that mysterious quality undoubtedly is a leader's ability to communicate major assumptions and values in a vivid and clear manner. . . ."

It's as hard to argue with that tautology as it is to apply it.

For most of this century, managers at America's foundational companies—say, General Motors, IBM, or AT&T— slowly ascended the proverbial career ladder, which offered on each rung new responsibilities and privileges in precise calibration with slowly accreting traditional knowledge about the firm's methods and markets. The key to the executive bathroom was a visible sign of grace in a world where there was a "GM way," an "IBM way," an "AT&T way" and all major problems had been solved.

The collapse of these command and control pyramids—

long satirized in books like *The Organization Man* and *The Man in the Gray Flannel Suit,* and plays like *How to Succeed in Business Without Really Trying*—was sudden and genuinely traumatic. Indeed, the turmoil that occurred from the late 1970s to the mid-1990s, when forty-three *million* corporate jobs were lost, was our nearest equivalent to the implosion of the centralized economies of the Communist bloc. In both cases, the size, complexity and sheer disorder of markets simply overwhelmed the adaptive capacities of rigid hierarchies.

In the most extraordinary chapter in this nation's commercial history, corporate America eliminated, merged or transformed itself, creating within two decades the most flexible and cost-efficient economy in existence. The point too often lost in analyses of this watershed event is that it didn't just *happen.* If companies had to be more agile, more responsive to and anticipatory of market movements, then someone had to be at the helm, charting a course, constantly responding to shifts in the commercial wind and weather. But there is an irreducible mystery surrounding the identity of this captain, and what precisely it is that induces his crew to follow him.

Yes, leadership moves organizations, which means people, in the direction leaders wish them to go. And yes, successful leaders are generally smart, focused, experienced, energetic, knowledgeable and competitive. But these descriptors identify operational competence, which is not uncommon, not leadership. The mystery here is the mystery of personality itself. What is it made of and why are some of us regarded as "likable" or "impressive" or as evoking loyalty and admiration in others? I recall reading several years ago of a man's promotion to a senior position in network television. He was the kind of executive, said someone quoted in the story, whom his subordinates "wanted to see succeed." Just what sort of person is that?

This conundrum is further complicated by the fact that leaders and certainly the figures in this book vary as much as individual character varies—which is to say infinitely. Adidas has done brilliantly under the aegis of a relaxed, congenial CEO who wanders around in stocking feet and old gym clothes, gradually feeding his mostly young and highly motivated lieutenants more and more power and autonomy. Chrysler thrives on the ongoing pas de deux of its CEO and president, two men of vastly different temperaments, whose example has inspired a rare company-wide spirit of collaboration in a business known for personal fiefdoms and turf wars. Compaq has achieved its present heady success under the baton of a disciplinarian conductor whose high competence and inflexible commitment allows him to insist upon and receive consistently remarkable performances from his entire orchestra. UPS found one of its own, the UPS man's UPS man, who managed to revolutionize his company by pretending that he was more of a traditionalist than anyone. Continental drafted a gruff-speaking, straight-shooting squadron leader to rebuild troop morale, devise a plan of attack and send them out into the battle for the commercial skies. And so on.

It seems to me that the lesson, despite an endless river of books, articles, lectures, seminars and wilderness retreats testifying to the contrary, is that there is no one true path to leadership. Further, that leadership itself is not a single thing, but as noted above, an affect, a public expression and an extension of one person's personality and intelligence—one's *being*. This may sound irritatingly New Age–ish, but give the proposition a moment's thought. Do people develop loyalty toward a position or a title? Do employees commit themselves headlong to the success of a cipher? I would argue, no.

In fact, remarkable leaders find a way to integrate their selves and the functions of their job, so that their colleagues daily find themselves interacting with a person, not a totem whose power to promote, demote or fire must be propitiated. It must also be recognized that, while there are many talented people, few of them truly wish to be leaders. Sure, everyone chafes under restraint. But this negative wish for autonomy or license is qualitatively different from the desire to bear ultimate responsibility and, in all candor, to control the fate of others. There is a close analogy here to sports, where team leaders are those who "want the ball" when the game is on the line. Most players would just as soon the ball went elsewhere, and their teammates know it.

This attraction to responsibility is possessed by all the capable leaders I have known, and in my view is one of their principal characteristics. The term "reluctant leader" strikes me as nonsense. Each of the men in this book found that, however it came, high position and authority struck a deep chord; it helped them to find and define themselves in the world. Nonetheless, I believe that only two or three of the men in this book *had* to become CEOs to achieve a good measure of vocational satisfaction. Indeed, several of them are perfectly comfortable sharing power with a virtual co-CEO. But modesty and authority are never in contradition. That cannot be said of real reluctance, which is disabling. A truly reluctant leader will not last. He or she will bail out or be thrown out, and probably be the happier for it.

A neurotic, Freud said, is a mind in conflict with itself. And a fair number of titular leaders are neurotic in just this way; they aspire, perhaps, to position and privilege, but in fact don't want to fully inhabit the job. That may mean that they don't want to interact with others all the time, or make difficult decisions, especially under pressure, or fire people or hire people. They may want to be responsible for their people and for the success of an enterprise *sometimes,* but that's not an option. They are like those men and women who only want to be parents some of the time, while reserving the right to unfettered liberty when it suits them. It's bad for children and bad for employees.

These sometime leaders almost certainly experience difficulty with the relentless self-exposure leadership demands, as well. You are always under a microscope, the object of all eyes and many thoughts. And if you try to hide from this scrutiny, like the Air Force doctor in *Catch 22,* who gives orders that he is never "in" when he's in his office, you cede the credibility and respect needed to do the job.

Beyond a desire for authority and an embrace of responsibility, the CEOs I've focused on, and virtually every leader I've known, display a determination to surround themselves with the brightest and most competent colleagues. Once again, there is an inner disposition at work here, a maturity that does not shy away from the challenge posed by gifted, ambitious people. But it's not just that. Harry Truman once said, "A leader is a man who has the ability to get other people to do what they don't want to do and like it." This has his characteristic homespun charm and conviction, but in today's world it's wrong. CEO Louis Gerstner apparently came to IBM with something like that in mind. He took office telling the world that all the company needed was a good kick in the pants—price things right, market them aggressively. A year later he told *The New York Times* that he had come to understand that IBM itself had to change, not just its products, and that changing a culture "is not something you do by writing memos. You've got to appeal to people's emotions. They've got to buy in with their hearts and their beliefs, not just their minds."

The contemporary leader's only reliable weapon against the constantly shifting market realities he faces is the best information and ideas, which can only come from colleagues whose skills and intelligence he respects and relies on. Edgar Schein, a professor of management at MIT, nicely captures this in a passage from the book *Organizational Culture and Leadership,* which he wrote with Cedric Crocker. Schein writes, ". . . the toughest problem for learning leaders is to come to terms with their own lack of expertise and wisdom. Once we are in a leadership position our own needs and the expectations of others dictate that we know the answers and be in control of the situation. Yet if we provide the answers, we are creating a culture that . . . will take a moralistic position in regard to reality and the truth. The only way to build a . . . culture that continues to learn is for leaders themselves to realize that they do not know and must teach others to accept that they do not know. The learning task is then a shared responsibility."

In other words, the truth does not come only out of certain mouths, and what they say is not, axiomatically, the *Truth*. To believe this entails a certain optimism regarding human potential, yet another trait of all those I've profiled. In 1960, Douglas MacGregor, another MIT management professor, wrote the famous text, *The Human Side of Enterprise*. MacGregor believed that the universe of managers could be divided in two. On one side were ineffective managers, who generally held to a worldview he called Theory X, the thrust of which was that people were basically lazy and had to be closely monitored, constantly prodded and carefully controlled. Effective managers, by contrast, gravitated toward Theory Y. "Y-ites" believed that people are self-motivated and need to be challenged, not controlled. Most fundamentally, Theory X implies that organizations and people are by nature in conflict; Theory Y, that they are in collaboration, or can be, given intelligent leadership.

MacGregor wasn't suggesting that successful leaders were Will Rogers types, who never met a man they didn't like, or even that they were necessarily convivial people, with rich social lives. Rather, it was that they had a certain faith in the capacities and responsiveness of people. This is the view explicitly stated by Robert Louis-Dreyfus in his profile, and it's implicit in the relations all the other CEOs here have with their colleagues. In every instance, there is a shared assumption that they are all "in this" together, and that they are all professional, all adults, all to be counted on in critical situations.

The qualities of intellect and character touched upon here will, I hope, offer a kind of touchstone to those who wish to exercise positive leadership themselves. The gifted people in this book may be extraordinary, but their example, to end where I began this book, can still give us "things we can use." In particular, would-be leaders need to ask themselves whether their behavior is such that it merits allegiance. In other words, *should* anybody follow them, given the evidence of their words and deeds and performance record. Are they mature enough, solid enough, to merit the faith and loyalty of their colleagues?

Perhaps, too, this book will help others to understand that leadership is not a goal, but a journey. There is an old proverb that the road is better than the inn, which everybody I've profiled would certainly agree with. Getting to the top is meaningless by itself; reaching for the top, which is ever-changing in its particulars, is the point of this particular road. As Howard Gardner and Emma Laskin write in *Leading Minds: An Anatomy of Leadership*, "No leader is ever fully realized; at most, one can observe individuals who are in the course of attaining greater skills and heightened effectiveness."

Edward Levy, the late dean of the University of Chicago Law School, taught a famous first-year course that began with his asking the question, "What is justice?" What followed were many opinions and much debate, but, of course, no conclusion. Justice is a goal and a hope and a necessity. But it is never static, never complete, and never fully defined. According to Deuteronomy, it's something we must *pursue*.

Leadership is like that, too. We need it, admire it and seek it. It can help provide a sense of excitement and challenge to daily existence, and define goals that give life meaning. A leader can help those he leads to anchor their

sense of self-worth in the solid ground of achievement encouraged, recognized and rewarded. But leadership, like
justice, never assumes final form and it is never done with
its work. There is always tomorrow and its challenges.

In the end, let us agree that leadership remains puz-
zling, fascinating, necessary and elusive. But let us also
agree that, unlike demagoguery or entertainment, it does
not seek to enlist followers in a fantasy of reality. Rather, it
invites us to struggle together toward the truth of things,
the real, which is a dignified goal and as good a way to live
and work as I can imagine.

INDEX